Real Estate Investing 101

Earnest Kelley

Noble House
Baltimore, Maryland

Real Estate Investing 101

Copyright © 2007 Earnest Kelley

Library of Congress
Cataloging-in-Publication Data
ISBN-10: 1-56167-953-4
ISBN-13: 978-1-56167-953-9

Library of Congress Card Catalog Number:
2006910025

Published by

8019 Belair Road, Suite 10
Baltimore, Maryland 21236

Manufactured in the United States of America

ACKNOWLEDGMENTS

This book is dedicated to my wonderful wife, Eva, my soul mate, for her immense patience and understanding.

Many evenings she sat alone watching TV while this book was being written.

My special thanks go to my daughter, Enez, for encouraging me to write this book based on my experiences.

DISCLAIMER

The opinions and recommendations given herein are based exclusively on the author's experience and on his research, which he believes to be accurate and reliable, but not infallible.

This publication is designed to provide general information and guidance in real estate investment. However, laws and practices vary from state to state, and are subject to change. Because of the inherent differences in each investment situation, specific advice should be tailored to the particular circumstances. For this reason, the reader is advised to consult with his or her own investment advisor regarding each specific situation.

The author has taken reasonable precautions in the preparation of this book and believes that the facts presented in the book are accurate as of the date it was written. However, neither the author nor the publisher assumes any responsibility for any errors or omissions. The author and publisher specifically disclaim any liability resulting from the use or application of the information contained in this book, and the information is not in any way intended to serve as legal or professional advice.

PREFACE

After serving twenty years in Military Service, I decided to go to college and improve myself intellectually. With the help of the GI Bill, I finished two years at Wilson Junior College in Chicago, Illinois. That's when I decided to fulfill my dream of becoming financially secure.

I moved to Detroit, Michigan, because I knew a few real estate agents there and had worked with some of them. After approximately six months, I obtained a real estate license in the state of Michigan, and began working with the Miller Brothers Real Estate Company.

Having the opportunity to work with successful real estate investors, I looked deep into their activities and methods. I gained valuable insight into their investment practices and saw how they actually made their fortunes through real estate investments. I decided right then and there that I too wanted to invest in real estate, and I set myself a goal to retire in four years.

During my career as a real estate broker, mortgage broker, and manager of my own properties, I made use of every opportunity to acquire valuable knowledge and experience in real estate investing, with the result that it literally propelled me from the work force into early retirement!

I must say that the discipline I acquired during military service had a deep-seated effect in enabling me to stay focused on my goal of retiring early.

The harder I worked, the better I liked the challenge, and the more the money kept coming in … wave after wave, after wave! I trust this book will help many families who are unaware that they can, with little effort, earn more than just their paychecks.

I am writing this book to reach out in a manner suitable for laymen on the bottom step of the investment ladder. I have provided my utmost attention to the needs of the beginner in real estate investing. My plan is to assist you in making your decision to increase your income to greater heights through real estate investing.

I urge you to do as I did in my early years of real estate investing. I focused on opportunities rather than problems. I learned how to build financial security in my life. I listened to real estate investors and read various publications. Reading books on real estate investments was an important step in my development as an investor, and it tremendously boosted my confidence.

From my analysis, the message I received loud and clear was to invest in real estate and manage my own properties. I gladly accepted the challenge and succeeded in reaching my goal within the four years I had planned, and retired at age 52!

I am enthusiastic in sharing my knowledge and experience with you! The strategies, techniques and tactics in this book will help you get started in the world of real estate. Reading and following the methods in this book will equip you with the knowledge and skills to succeed!

As your knowledge increases, so will your potential for accumulating wealth. The degree of wealth a person possesses at any given time reflects the degree of knowledge that propelled that person to reach such a financial position.

I am forever thankful to God for having guided me in the right direction, and this book represents my honest effort to give something back to the community!

Remember, give kindness without expecting any in return, and the rewards will flow back to you!

TABLE OF CONTENTS

Chapter		*Page*
1	Getting Started	1
2	The Beginner Investor	13
3	Getting Support	27
4	Finding Sellers	37
5	Negotiating	45
6	Funding	53
7	Tenants	61
8	Rental Income	69
9	Rent or Sell	75
10	Good Faith Settlement Cost	85
11	Property Management	95
12	Nuts and Bolts of a Home Inspection	101
13	A Map for Your Retirement Future	107
	Appendices	113
	Acceptance of Partial Payment and Non-Waiver Agreement	*114*
	Property Interior Checklist	*115*
	Property Exterior Checklist	*118*
	Hold Harmless Agreement for Moving Tenant	*119*
	Notice of Termination	*120*
	Three-Day Notice	*121*
	Seven-Day Notice	*122*
	Security Deposit Refund Sheet	*123*
	Tenant Move-Out Sheet	*124*
	Addendum	*125*
	Notice of Dishonored Check	*127*
	Notice of Intention to Impose Claim on Security Deposit	*128*
	Lead-Based Paint or Lead-Based Paint Hazard Addendum	*129*
	Warranty Deed	*130*
	Authorization to Release Loan Information	*131*
	Quit-Claim Deed	*132*
	Glossary	133
	Index	147

CHAPTER ONE
GETTING STARTED

Real estate has long been a proven path for making millions of dollars in a very short period of time. Almost anyone can walk along this path. Getting started is the most difficult part for the beginner in real estate ‚investing. First, you must plan … and plan … and plan. The difference between planning and dreaming is slippery, but real planning is a plan that embodies diligent action. Planning also gives you hope, and hope in return gives you faith. Hope without faith is like a beefsteak without taste.

Set up some well-defined plans before you start an investment regimen. Of course, you cannot formulate all of your plans in one sitting or in one week. You must begin by giving strong consideration to your capital assets, your age, and your family situation. Make a draft of your plans, and then go over and refine them. Dreams put into action through planning are essential to the accumulation of wealth!

Vividly picture your desired goal in your conscious mind, and focus on that picture until it actually sinks into your unconscious mind! Believe that your goal is your own prized possession, and that there is no doubt that it will come to pass. If you put forth effective action, it is certain to lead you down the path to success. All you have to do is open the door, and your goals will be gazing squarely in your smiling face! It was said of J. P. Morgan, the famous successful industrialist and financier, that "he had the genius to focus all his mental powers and concentrate on one thing for five minutes!"

BELIEVE AND SUCCEED!

Believe and succeed is the simple law of achieving prosperity! To truly believe is the ability to have a firm religious faith that investment property is within your reach. Many people fail to move forward with their buying plans for investment property because of their own psychological barriers. These barriers show up when people are not clear about what they want and how to take steps to pursue their dreams. They freeze, and are unable to act.

They may say, "Oh my God! There's no way I can find that kind of money to invest in rental property." Some people, because of their low self-esteem, believe that they don't deserve the financial success they really want. Thus, the barriers preventing you from achieving a more fulfilling lifestyle are self-imposed!

Jesus Christ said:

"What things so ever ye desire, when you pray, believe that ye receive them, and ye shall have them." (Mark 11:24)

When you vividly picture a desired goal in your conscious mind and believe it is yours, you have just prayed and it will come to pass; if you put forth some constructive efforts, you will receive it. Vividly picturing something in your mind is what causes the connection to take place between your inner self and God. Believe it or not, such innate powers exist in every human being on the face of the earth!

Teach yourself to think positively about everything you do, and move toward your goal with deep expectation of accomplishment! When you adopt this attitude, things will begin to happen in your favor almost at once. A law recognized by psychologists around the world involves changing your mentality to believe instead of disbelieve. Learn to expect, not to doubt. With this new attitude, you'll bring everything you desire into the realm of accessibility!

Rely on your instincts, especially when you are negotiating various kinds of real estate deals. If the situation does not feel right, or if you instinctively feel like you're dealing with a crook, trust your instincts and back off.

THINK POSITIVE!

Watch out when you moan and groan about the conditions you're facing—your finances, your job, your neighbor, or even your weight. You may unknowingly be harming not only yourself but everyone in sight or hearing by passing along harmful attitudes about achieving financial success. You can help yourself and everyone around you by being a positive thinker!

"So as a man thinkest, so is he." (Proverbs 23-7).

Do not be defeated by everyday problems or go through life with a sense of resentment of what you consider "bad breaks" that life has given you. Remember, there is a spirit and a method by which we all can control and even determine our destiny. We have control over three main aspects of our lives: what to say, what to think, and how to behave!

To make meaningful changes in your life, you must come to the realization that you own and control the powers to shape your financial future. When you exercise these powers in ways that benefit you and your family, you'll be happier, smarter, more assertive, and more independent, just to mention a few of the numerous benefits.

Don't let your ego give you an inflated view of yourself. You may think you are in a rational mode of thinking when in fact you are taking comfort in being part of the norm. For instance, if everyone is buying townhouses, it must be okay; and if you lose money that way, well, at least you are no dumber than everyone else. Investors tend to overestimate the value of a small amount of knowledge, and gain confidence from it. Don't be misled by an inflated ego; think clearly.

PSYCHOLOGICAL FLAWS

Sigmund Freud (1856-1939), an Austrian physician, was the founder of psychoanalysis. Freud inspired people around the world to consider the effects of the unconscious mind. Studies show that we all have psychological flaws embedded in our unconscious mind. For instance, we tend to place more value on things we own than on things we do not. Therefore, we stick with investments we have rather than go for more productive ones.

How can you overcome the built-in psychological flaws? By realizing they are there, and by positive thinking that will stoke your ego in a realistic direction. For instance, you may say, "I'm going to invest in real estate; I hope I'll be successful." Or you may say, "I'm going to invest in real estate, and I know I will be successful." Positive thinking creates positive imaging, and positive imaging instills faith, thereby changing that negative image of yourself from a faithless loser to something else–a positive winner. If you do choose the latter, your unconscious mind will respond in a favorable direction. And once your unconscious mind takes hold of that positive idea, you will find yourself being swept along by a current flowing wave after wave after wave, from the arid desert of doubt to the green fields of prosperity.

HAVE CONFIDENCE IN YOURSELF!

Confidence begets confidence. Confidence will generate faith that you will act in a responsible way that will lead you to your goal. Without a sound, confident base within yourself, you cannot be successful or happy. A sense of inferiority or inadequacy interferes with the attainment of your hopes, but self-confidence leads to self-realization and successful achievement!

Your easy, relaxed, confident mannerisms will encourage sellers to relax and talk more freely about their property. When you exude confidence and appear to have an interest in the sellers' and their families' well-being, they become more willing to assert themselves in a positive manner.

They will speak in a manner that makes it obvious they are willing to take a reduced price for their property, or they may indicate they will not budge from their asking price. Whatever it may be, so be it. At least you'll know enough to choose the best strategy to implement, and the best time to make your move.

One of the most powerful concepts that is a sure cure for lack of confidence is the positive thought that God is actually with you and helping you! This idea is so powerful in developing self-confidence and so simple to practice. Visualize God's presence and say, "God is with me... God is with me!"

BENDING THE RULES

Many beginner real estate investors think they can bend the rules or do whatever they like and call it "their style." However, there are some firm principles in the business world!

Investing in real estate is a business, and it is wise to observe customary expectations in business circles. As you climb the ladder and get more familiar with the rules and expectations of your lenders, mortgage brokers and real estate agents, you will become more adept in following the rules. You will also gain a better understanding of where you can bend the rules and still get away with it. In your early years, be sure you are attentive to the established ways of conduct, behavior, and methods, and stick to the traditional expectations! Later on, you can think about breaking the mold!

OPPORTUNITY

Now is the time for you to seize your opportunity to invest in real estate! In just a short time, you can elevate your income to great heights by following the examples set forth in this book. If you're wondering how one person seems to get elevated financially over another with no apparent rhyme or reason, I've got the answer. It is by making use of opportunity! And you have full access to it!

Opportunity is in the unseen current that moves you wave after wave after wave from your present situation to the destiny and goals you're focused on!

Opportunity will do for you what your money, your personality, your abilities, and your career cannot do. Opportunity takes you from ordinary to extraordinary, and thus gives you chances for advancement or progress. I believe we should make every effort to simply take advantage of every opportunity that opens up to us within the direction of the goals we have in mind. All you need to do is take advantage of the opportunity that confronts you and excel!

Opportunity is the rarely taught principle of the art or practice of taking advantage of favorable situations for financial advantage. It is difficult for us to comprehend in our finite minds how opportunities masterfully orchestrate our lives with a multitude of blessings that we fail to access because we do not recognize them or we think we do not deserve them and cannot earn them. Yet opportunity is all around you! There is no scarcity of opportunity to advance in every aspect of your life. There is only a scarcity of effort to make successful results happen. Your success depends on taking advantage of opportunities that favor your objectives and plans.

For example, you may learn that a shopping center will be built near your area. This may be an opportunity. You check the plans and zoning in your area and find that a shopping center is being constructed near you— an opportunity. You take off like a big bird and search for vacant land suitable for apartments or commercial buildings, or for single family houses that can be converted to a duplex or fourplex (two or four units). Put as many purchase offers as you can on properties, developed or undeveloped. Later, you can sell the property for a higher price or develop it for rental property. In any case, you'll have plenty of time to wriggle.

BEING LUCKY

Being lucky is nothing more than being in the right place at the right time and knowing what to do next. You can get ahead big time in the real estate industry by utilizing your gift of opportunities (and not a rabbit's foot)!

CREATE YOUR OWN LUCK!

Talk to people in the workplace, or even to strangers. Simple conversations can turn into great opportunities or generate fantastic ideas. You never know whom you will meet or where the conversation will lead. Make some small talk. Take a personal interest, especially in the other person's point of view. Take time to know the people you see every day. When they ask how you are, draw close to them and give them a pleasant answer with a question like, how are you? They may drop names. Name dropping isn't necessarily bragging about how well-connected they are.

Finding a friend or acquaintance in common creates a more personal connection and opens doors. Don't be reluctant about eavesdropping and listening. Be aware of everything that goes on around you. You could be in a good position to ask for or offer help. It's also a fantastic way to learn about opportunities to increase your cash flow.

THE STATUS QUO

Don't just stick to the *status quo*. Stray from the beaten path! As I said before, opportunities are all around. Use your skills for success, not just the ones you're learning in this book. Also, remember that relationships can turn sour, so know when to zip your lip and make a gracious exit without burning bridges. Exit on a high, pleasant note so that you will have room to wriggle back in with respect if you choose to do so.

Remember, as long as we are breathing on this earth, we are going to encounter a mixture of things we like ... and don't like. We are going to be surrounded by a mixture of people who make us feel warm all over, and people who are difficult to be near.

THE FIRST IMPRESSION

Believe it or not, ***you only get one chance to make a first impression!*** According to some experts, the first four minutes of a first meeting are crucial. While this may sound an unbelievably brief amount of time in which to make a lasting judgment about another person, some experts argue it is actually even shorter!

They believe that an enduring evaluation is often made within the first hundred twenty seconds of an encounter, and this applies whether you're trying to impress an attractive new companion, trying to impress a mortgage lender, or trying to convince a seller to take a first mortgage with a low down payment.

In any business deal, making a good first impression could mean the difference between landing the deal or heading back to the drawing board! Your posture, eye contact, listening skills, and of course, the way you smile, are all critical to the first impression you make.

DRESS

Only two types of people can get away with ignoring social expectations when it comes to what they wear: the super fat-cats who have nothing to prove, and the super poor who have nothing to lose. For the rest of us, dressing for success is a matter of great importance indeed. Always remember that what you wear reflects an impression. Dress according to the kind of impression you would like to create!

A DONE DEAL

Did your first impression leave a good mark on that mortgage lender?

If you are saying goodbye to your mortgage lender after a meeting in his or her office, and he or she walks you at least as far as the door, this interaction emphasizes the value placed on the relationship. If they escort you even farther, such as to the elevator, that action shows the intensity of their feelings of acceptance and empathy!

You might say it's a done deal!

SELF-ESTEEM

One way of making a favorable impact is to make certain that the level of your self-esteem is matched to the individual whose impression you wish to control. If you are in a group, match your level of self-esteem to that of the most influential person present.

Projecting a successful self-image demands perception, confidence, and the ability to control your emotions, such as anxiety or irritation.

SMILE

A smile must be open and friendly. A smile is the universal language that opens doors, melts defenses, and saves a thousand words. A smile is the light in your heart that tells others there is a caring, sharing person inside you!

WHAT YOU FOCUS ON IS WHAT YOU GET!

We act upon our thoughts. Whatever you're thinking about and focusing on in a serious, deep-seated way will inevitably become your principle. Consequently, if you are focusing on scarcity for long periods of time, scarcity is what you'll get.

Never operate from a mentality of scarcity when it concerns your prosperity. Have your goals firmly fixed in your mind. You should be able to see each goal as plainly as you can see your hands in front of you. When we focus on our goals and when we operate from the principle of prosperity, we generally believe we are happy, loved, and our basic needs are met.

Our world is abundantly full of good things. How we think of them is our choice!

Sometimes, it feels like life is a tug of war and we are the rope. When you feel overwhelmed and frustrated, remember to take things one at a time. Stay focused on your goals, and remain excited about the financial security that awaits you!

Most importantly, stay focused!

SUCCESSFUL INVESTORS

Successful real estate investors are very aware of their environment and plans. They are aware of the things they don't know and are eager to learn, especially about their own personal contributions to the plans they constantly have in focus.

Understand that self development is a lifetime program and is embodied in a positive perception. Successful investors are goal and role-oriented, and have been known to work hard, even holding second jobs to get what they want!

We become what we think most of the time of becoming! Whatever we are thinking of now is what we are unconsciously moving toward with the achievement of that thought! For an alcoholic, it may be the next drink.

For a drug addict, it is probably the next fix; for the surfer, the next wave.

Divorce and bankruptcy are spawned out of negativity and habitually focusing on negative patterns. We all have the potential and opportunity for success in our lives. It takes just as much energy and effort for an unsuccessful life as it does for a good, successful life. Yet, many people wouldn't know the opportunity for a happy life if it was standing in front of them with the door open, and there are many who may notice it but never enter! They exist from day to day, year to year, paycheck to paycheck. They have never made the decision to seek ways to increase their income. They sit back in their conference rooms and never move forward with plans to increase their income.

Thomas Carlyle and Earl Nightingale both compare human beings to ships.

"About 95% can be compared to ships without rudders, subject to every shift of wind and tide, they are helplessly adrift. And while they fondly hope that they'll one day drift into a rich and successful port, they usually end up on the rocks or run aground.

But the five percent who have taken the time and exercised the discipline to decide on a destination and to chart a course and sail wave after wave after wave, straight and far reaching, one port after another, accomplish more in just a few years than the rest accomplish in a lifetime!"

Most people spend more time planning a party, watching TV, or making a Christmas list than they do planning their lives. (What a shame!)

ATTITUDE OF THE MIND

Where the mind goes, man follows. Your attitude is the criteria for success in any endeavor. How many people in life have rejected their genetic handicap and ventured out of their comfort zone into a new dimension where their self-esteem and the esteem of others produce results?

Attitude is the answer. Your attitude toward your goals is either the key to, or the lock on the door to your personal financial security. Your total individual behavioral and emotional characteristics are imbedded in your attitude.

William James, one of America's most profound psychologists, was a leader in the study of the human mind. He said:

"The greatest discovery of my generation is that human beings

can alter their lives by altering the attitudes of their minds."

In order to feel good, confident, assertive, creative, and motivated to excel, you need to get your attitude in harmony with constructive thinking in order to "till the soil" so that positive thoughts can take root, to play your own ballgame.

In the real estate industry, let your attitude be your coach and play it as you would play to win. There are no practice games dealing with mortgage lenders, real estate brokers, mortgage brokers, or real estate sellers.

It's your playoff!

Learn the principles!

Alter the attitude of your mind, and win!

MOTIVATION

How many times have you heard people say of someone, "He is not motivated?" Whatever behavior we observe, we are seeing the motivational process in action. Motivation is indeed the action part of a need-satisfaction cycle. Whatever need you have, consciously or subconsciously, at any given moment will cause a type of behavior, and your action, activity, or reaction can be associated with the perceived eventual satisfaction of the need.

Motivation, for the most part, is an individual matter. However, input from other people, groups or situations affect a person's motives. Since people act and interact with other people, motivated behavior is often part of a social process. The basic considerations are fundamental to understanding human behavior. People engage in behaviors that they believe will satisfy their needs. In effect, you should be motivated to serve your own interests in the real estate investment world.

It is good and rewarding to motivate yourself by serving your own interests as long as the activities you pursue and the behaviors you exhibit are legal, moral, and ethical. The rewards you seek may be physical, social, psychological, real estate or some combination thereof. The larger the cost, the larger the expected reward. The bottom line is: Most people fail to motivate themselves by refusing to set goals to meet their deep desires. Therefore, most people just get by financially from paycheck to paycheck. The fact is, people determine their own destiny, and any person who refuses to grasp that fact is doomed to failure and weakness ...

MOVE TO ACTION

Motivation is the force that moves us to action, and it springs from inside the individual. It cannot be pumped in from incentives, pep talks, contests, encouragements and aspirations for anyone to turn on creative powers. People will be motivated only if they want to. Motivational powers enter the conscious and become effective only when the need for change is understood and accepted. Motivation does not have to be inborn. It can be learned and developed. You can motivate yourself.

CHAPTER TWO
THE BEGINNER INVESTOR

Real estate is land and all the things ultimately attached to it, such as the trees, the buildings upon it and any minerals such as oil, coal, iron, or gas beneath the surface.

Therefore, when you buy real estate you not only get what you see, you also get what you don't see!

The term "real property" came into use from the fact that, in case of contest over the title, the rightful owner received the real property. This was not necessarily true in the contest over the ownership of chattels, which might be settled by a payment of money.

The realization of the value of real estate entered the consciousness of man when Adam and Eve had to till the land and grow their food. From that stage, they may have realized the value of land to live on and grow fruit and vegetables, and the need to own and protect it. Later, man perceived that he could invest in land, build a home on it, grow crops on a larger scale, raise livestock, and produce meat, grain, fruit and vegetables to market for a profit.

STALLED PAYCHECK

Many people's paychecks are stalled at almost the same level as when they started working. Many are looking for ways to enhance their income by getting involved in some kind of income-producing activity. Although many innovative opportunities are within their reach, what they need is an idea compass to point them in the right direction.

This book is your compass, and real estate investment is your opportunity!

Once you zero in on a good income-producing property, you'll know whether your compass is working, and if the compass needle is pointing in the right direction, telling you to go ahead, go ahead and seize the opportunity!

You can do it, and I can help you get results!

BUYER INVESTOR

According to a survey by the National Association of Realtors, almost one in four real estate sales in the United States involves buyers seeking an investment rather than a place to live.

Investors are also a lot more conservative than you might have heard. Many of them opt to put an average of 20% down, which makes loans to such investors low risk. Investors keep their purchases within ten miles of each other, making hands-on control easier. Their goals are to find properties to produce a steady income stream to enhance their paychecks, or for full income.

Many of my clients had both an IRA and a 401(k). They liked the idea of investing in real estate to supplement their retirement income.

What's so appealing about real estate investment?

One good thing is being able to acquire property using other people's money (OPM) and getting all the benefits from the investment.

Experts say, and I agree, that real estate is a lot more stable than many investment options out there, and it is accessible to anyone. *See Chapter Four.*

PREPARATION

Before entering our diverse, competitive real estate market, you must learn how to prepare yourself for the exciting challenge that awaits you. Remember, real estate, innovative activities, and interactions are not a single event. They are ongoing processes—deal, after deal, after deal—and money flows in wave after wave after wave!

Before you follow any kind of compass needle, it is wise to prepare yourself in a way that gives you a solid foundation in such an ongoing process.

Remember, knowledge is not found in books. Books contain information, whereas knowledge includes the ability to apply information to specific work and performance.

When real estate investors are ignorant about the needs of prospective tenants and sellers, the prospective tenants think the investor is looking out just for himself or herself. In other words, the investors are interested only in what they can get from the situation, not how they can help the prospective tenants' situation. Experts agree that real estate investors who have done their homework in finding out how a particular transaction will also help or attract others will get ahead faster every time!

Preparation is the key. Get what I mean?

THE SMALL INVESTOR

Small investors with little or no capital can successfully use the same principles and strategies that the fat-cats use. It is not the scale of your real estate investment that counts. It doesn't matter if you are investing in a single-family home, a four-family, or in multimillion dollar office complex. What is important is your knowledge and the investment strategies you use to acquire and develop the property!

Of course, how to design and market the property to potential tenants and buyers is important too. As a matter of fact, whether you are a small investor or just beginning, you may have a big advantage in many areas. For instance, if you are shooting for a rate of return of 15%, 25%, or even 75%, as a small investor you can compound your money at these higher rates because of the amount of money you're working with. Consider this example:

A neighbor of mine came to me and told me that "his friend was selling his house." I asked him how big the house was, one or two units. I said I was not interested in single-family houses. I was buying two, three and four-family houses. He said, "Well, if he doesn't sell, the house will be foreclosed." My brain began to function in overdrive. I envisioned the "don't-want-to sell" seller and the "anxious" seller all in one!

I immediately made an appointment to see the house. It was a modest, well-kept house, located in a middle-class area in Detroit, Michigan, on the northwest side. I knew the asking price of $90,000 was about right for a house in that area. To my surprise, the owner said he had to sell before the house foreclosed and therefore was lowering the price to $85,000. I offered him $84,000 cash. And he accepted my offer!

I went directly home and called my bank!

My account was already set up so that I could get quick access to money when I needed it. They knew all about me and what kind of business I was doing. The next day, after signing a stack of papers, I picked up a money order for $84,000. Six days later, I went to the closing, paid the $84,000, plus a small amount for closing costs. I took title using other people's money! The basement made a big one-bedroom, one-bath and kitchen apartment. In approximately three months, through my bank, I got an $89,000, 30-year, fixed-rate mortgage with "0" down. I paid off the balance of the $84,000.00 note, and after paying various kinds of interest, I put $3,016.00 in my pocket!

Rental income on this property was as follows:

Main house	$ 925.00
Basement apartment	$ 675.00
Garage apartment	$ 585.00
Income	**$2,185.00**
Less: Note	$ 910.00
Cash Flow	**$1,275.00**

All upkeep and utilities were paid by tenants, who also undertook maintenance of the yard. The tenants agreed that my handyman was allowed to inspect the property anytime between 8:00 a.m. and 4:00 p.m. Monday through Saturday.

Here's a method I learned from George Jennings, an associate of mine when I worked with Miller Brothers Realty Company in Detroit, concerning a four-unit residential property: The owner wanted a large down payment. Everything else was just fine, even the expected cash flow. The property was in poor condition, but nothing major such as a new roof. Due to the poor condition, the seller was asking $16,000 with a 25% down payment. I made a full price offer with 25% down, the balance to be carried by the seller on a second mortgage, allowing me to put a first mortgage on it at the time of closing.

I went to my bank and secured a first mortgage to close exactly at the same time that I closed on the property. The amount of the first mortgage was $20,000, $4,000 of which would be paid to the seller at the time of closing. The total price was $16,000. This left the balance of $12,000.

Now here is the good part. This deal puts $16,000 in my pocket to buy another property. I spent approximately $6,000 to fix up this property, but I still had $10,000 to purchase another property. After I fixed up the house, it was worth more than $29,000, and the end result was my strong point in getting the lender to lend me $20,000 on a $16,000 purchase!

BUYING STRATEGIES FOR THE BEGINNER

You may or may not own a home. However, you can easily get started building your wealth with income properties. Select a high LTV (loan-to-value) loan program that appeals to you. Then, buy a one, two, three or four-family property. Live in it until you find another property to buy. Then, rent it out and repeat the process.

After financing, the loan can remain on the property even after you move out. The second, third, and even fourth home you buy and move into will still qualify for the LTV financing. If you really like your current home, no problem. Rent out your most recently acquired property and move back into your former residence!

ONE YEAR AND ONE DAY

For all loan-to-value financing, you must tell the lender that you intend to live in the property for at least one year. Remember, intent does not guarantee anything. You can, for no reason at all, change your mind at any time, even before you leave the closing table. I clearly remember telling a closing agent, "I'll live there as long as it takes me to clean up the place." The closing agent smiled and said nothing, and I remained in my primary residence during all my LTV deals!

VA MORTGAGES

Believe it or not, I used my VA loan on two occasions. The first property I purchased, I sold in about one year. The second one, I sold the property in approximately four years. If you or anyone in your family has veteran benefits, you should own rental property. Easy qualifying, and little or no cash to close is the name of the game. This is a good seed to plant, one that will produce many money trees if planted in good soil! Good luck veterans!

ASSUMPTIONS

All VA loans may be assumed by veterans or non-veterans who qualify. Find a VA seller with little equity in his or her home, and you can get all the goodies with little or no down payment.

REVERSE MORTGAGES

If you are 62 years old or older, you may consider a reverse mortgage. If a husband and wife hold joint title, both owners must be 62. Even if this is not for you because of your age, you may recommend this kind of deal to a friend, relative or seller. I suggested a reverse mortgage to my sister a few years ago. Today she's very happy with the total situation!

ADVANTAGES

A reverse mortgage offers a few disadvantages and many, many advantages for qualified home owners.

LIFETIME OR LUMP SUM

You can receive either monthly income or lump sums for any purchase, such as a new roof, new car, trip around the world, bill payoffs, a credit line (except in Texas, the big hat state), or any combination. The credit line is the most popular choice. In 2004, the volume of new reverse mortgages again set records, and the trend is expected to continue in 2006, especially because the three nationwide reverse mortgage lenders recently increased their lending limits.

NO MONTHLY PAYMENTS

The great feature going for a homeowner with a reverse mortgage is that there are no monthly payments. Even if you live to the age of 120, no repayment is required as long as you live in your principal residence, house or condo. Thus, a reverse mortgage is the opposite of the traditional home mortgage, which requires monthly payments from the borrower to the lender.

PAYMENT FLOW FROM LENDER TO BORROWER

A reverse mortgage creates payments flowing from the lender to the borrower. No repayment is required until either the borrower sells the home, the borrower dies, or the borrower has not lived in the home for more than twelve months. Only the residence is liable for eventual repayment of a reverse mortgage.

Contrary to widespread myth, the reverse mortgage lender does not take title to the home, nor can the lender ever force the senior citizens out of the home. To qualify for a senior citizen reverse mortgage, the property must be an owner-occupied, single-family house, condominium, or a manu-factured house on the owner's lot. Ineligible properties include vacation, second and rental houses, houseboats, mobile homes, commercial prop-erties, and farms (unless the residence is on a separate lot).

Lenders base eligibility on the age of the youngest spouse who holds title. Therefore, to get the highest monthly lifetime payment, the younger spouse simply quitclaims his/her interest in the property to the older spouse. Then the reverse mortgage eligibility will be much higher, based on the title holder with highest age.

RENEGOTIATE FOR A HIGHER AMOUNT

Reverse mortgages are frequently refinanced due to rising property values and declining interest rates. However, be aware, there will be new refinancing costs just as incurred on the original mortgage.

FIRST MORTGAGE

Reverse mortgages must be recorded as first mortgages. Any existing mortgage must be paid off, usually with a lump sum.

LENDERS

Most home mortgage lenders do not offer reverse mortgages. The largest nationwide reverse mortgage lenders are Financial Freedom Plan, Wells Fargo Mortgage, Seattle Mortgage, and GMAC. The best place to find local reverse mortgage originators is on the Internet at www.reversemortgage.org, then click on your state.

SAVINGS

Money is a prerequisite element in almost all real estate transactions. However, as I pointed out, there are some occasions when you will, with hard work, deep concentration, and creative financial thinking be in the right place at the right time. You'll come across some unbelievably good deals with no money down, and in a few cases leave the closing with money in your pocket from the closing proceeds. But believe me, such encounters are rare indeed.

Don't depend on the "no money down" mentality, but grab them when you come across them (and there will be a few).

Depend on money coming in from cash flows, loans from a bank, and from your savings to reinvest in property, and you'll progress much faster. Nothing down can help you get started in real estate, but only physical discipline can pave the way for long-term wealth and financial security. Before you consider looking for creative financing, direct your mentality to your own habits of spending, borrowing and saving. To get a good savings program going in your life, you may have to change your lifestyle and buckle down. Money will run out of your pocket like water from a faucet unless you take control and stop the flow.

Changing your lifestyle may cause you to lose cohesiveness with those who are clad in emotional armor and immune to your perception of becoming financially independent.

Sometimes, a friend or even a relative does not feel appreciated because you've changed your lifestyle from a happy-go-lucky spender to a thrift ideology lifestyle. He or she may play you against others, causing unpleasant friction in the family or social group. Play the game if you want to keep the peace, but keep your money in the cookie jar, and stay the course. Keep your focus. Sooner or later, you'll feel the tide turning in your favor, wave after wave after wave. And you'll laugh all the way to the bank.

PUT A CAP ON SPENDING

Put a cap on spending, and don't enter into any long-term contracts other than real estate investments. Maximize your savings and limit your buying to absolutely necessary things. It is important to put your money in assets with a lasting value, such as a home, investment property, money market certificates, or CDs (for certificates of deposit, see your banker).

Your quality of life need not suffer simply because you've decided to reduce your spending and save more money. If you are employed, consider saving at least 10% of your paycheck, and if you receive any extra income from any other source, put all that extra money in your savings and never, never take it out unless it is for the purpose of investing. If you think it will be over a year before you have capital to invest, you may consider putting your money in a short-term CD.

SLASH FOOD COSTS

There are many ways to save money, and many more if you are really serious about doing so. You may consider this method or suggest it to a friend: Through systematic comparison shopping, you can cut your food bill in half, still eat well, eat nutritional meals, and you probably won't lose weight. Buy a notebook and use one page for each of the seventy or so food and paper products that you buy routinely, then, as you go through the various stores, whether supermarkets, warehouses or superstores, jot down the best available price on the appropriate page. When your store price book is complete, you'll see which stores offer the best for each product.

Use the price book to assemble shopping lists, and save!

SAVE ON CAR BUYING

If you absolutely need (not want) a new car, here's some advice that you may also consider giving to your lending agent, mortgage agent, or your bank manager. Here is my strategy: First, decide the exact specifications of the model you want. Then, go to the Internet or a library and read a new car buying guide. Determine the dealer's cost for that car, then send letters to a dozen or more dealers in your area offering to buy the car for just $600 over the dealer's cost. I used this technique and several dealers responded to my query. Not only did I get rock-solid bids, but I was also spared the haggling. If you are in the market for a used car, then here are three web sites that feature information about used cars that can help you or a friend:

Car Buying Tips: www.carbuyingtips.com covers a wide range of used car buying topics.

Edmunds: www.Edmunds.com/caradvice.

The Federal Trade Commission: www.FTC.gov provides information on sale of IRS and seized automobiles.

SAVE ON HOME INSURANCE

In most states (check with your insurance company), homeowners can get big discounts on their premiums with upgrades to their property. If any of your properties have the right stuff, such as strong roofs and protected windows and doors, you can save up to 30% on your windstorm policy. You may also be able to lower premiums if you're upgrading your older home's electric wiring or plumbing. Don't be surprised if getting these discounts involves a home inspection. Home insurance companies are increasingly requesting these inspections, particularly on older homes.

CHECK OUT YOUR HOME

Check out your home, especially the roof. The shape of the property's roof can earn a property owner instant savings. If the slope upward is gentle, there is less resistance to the wind flowing over the house. Building engineers and construction experts say that a gable roof offers less resistance to the wind because it creates a high vertical surface on the two sides. Thus, the roof that offers less wind resistance is a good asset. Roofing additions such as straps that attach trusses to the frame, storm shutters providing resistance, stronger types of windows and doors, all play a part in reducing insurance costs!

STORM SHUTTERS

Insurers tend to consider storm shutters—metal or the clear ones—equally when it comes to discounting. Once the inspector signs off on the inspection and sends the documents to the insurer, you can expect discount considerations up to 30% depending on the situation. While insurers are particularly vigilant about demanding inspections on homes fifty years or older, even newer homes can benefit from an inspection because the review will find features that homeowners do not realize qualify for discounts, such as garage door openers, door fasteners, trimming back the larger trees standing close to the house, and entrance doors that open out instead of in. If you own three or more properties, you may save quite a lot.

SAVE ON INTEREST!

You can save big-time on interest by paying a little extra every month. On a $100,000 mortgage at 6% fixed rate for 30 years, you'll pay nearly $116,000 in interest. Put an extra $100 a month into principal payments, and you would pay just $76,000 and be done with mortgage payments nine years earlier! Moreover, that $100 a month could go into some other investment and perhaps do better. If the return on the alternative is higher than the mortgage rate, say 10% a year versus 6%, the alternative will earn more. However, the 6% "return" with the mortgage is guaranteed with no risk. I think the best alternative to the extra mortgage payment is the bank CD. They are government-insured and they don't lose value if interest rates rise.

Check CD and mortgage rates at www.bankrates.com and see the effect of extra principal payments at www.hsh.com/calcamort.html.

FINDING OUT THE CASH FLOW AND VALUE CAN BE FUN!

Your primary concern in protecting the growth or your net worth should be the return on equity (the return you get from investing money in real estate).

There are four basic kinds of returns on investment property:

1. Cash flow: money left over after all expenses including mortgage payments have been paid.
2. Equity buildup: results as mortgage payments gradually reduce the loan.
3. Tax savings: come via the favorable tax advantage of owning real estate (tax shelter).
4. Appreciation: develops as property increases in value over time and with improvements.

Before you buy an investment property, you should analyze the property's potential with respect to the above four kinds of investment returns. You'll discover some very interesting figures that will help you decide whether or not you should invest in a particular property. For example, you have discovered a four-unit property selling at $120,100 with $10,000 as a down payment. Now consider the four methods used to analyze any property in terms of its investment values.

1. CASH FLOW: It is simple to calculate the cash flow figure. Cash flow gives you, the investor, what is called a compounding effect on your money, and it can have a tremendous positive effect on the rate of growth in reaching your goals.

$$\frac{\text{Annual Cash Flow}}{\text{Down Payment}} = \frac{\$720}{\$10,000} = 7.2 \text{ percent}$$

The amount of cash on cash return appears to be a little low. Continue and observe the following three calculations.

2. EQUITY BUILDUP adds to your wealth as the monthly payments of $1,098 are made (from monthly income from tenants), and a portion of that goes toward the reduction of the $110,000 loan. You may determine that, at the end of the first year and after paying interest, your loan balance will drop to $109,156. If you decide to exit (sell) the property at this stage, you would pocket the $844 in principal reduction, plus

appreciation. This is known as a return on investment amounting to 8.4 percent:

$$\frac{\text{Loan Principal Reduction}}{\text{Down Payment}} = \frac{\$844}{\$10,000} = 8.4 \text{ percent}$$

3.   TAX SAVINGS: Real estate is the remaining economically sound tax shelter. The government has encouraged investors to invest in real estate for business purposes, and it permits investors to calculate a degree of wearing out of the buildings (but not of the land), which therefore lose value from year to year over the life of ownership. This process is called "depreciation." It relates to real estate and is an accounting expense.

Depreciation is an expense that you are allowed to deduct from the income of the building after all other expenses have been deducted. After depreciation is deducted, the property will no longer show a profit (for tax purposes only). The property often shows a good-sized loss, and that loss can be deducted from all income, including salary and income from other investments. In our example, the cost of the investment was $120,100. However, only a certain percentage of the cost is allowed to be attributed to the building. The remainder must be allocated to the land on which the building stands. In this example, the county tax assessment shows that, for county tax purposes, 80% of the value is attributed to the building and 20% to the land. Therefore, we can determine that the building has an assessed value of $96,000 ($120,000 x .80), and the land is worth $24,000. Keep in mind that the IRS says that land cannot be depreciated. Because of that, you should place the lowest possible value on the land that you can in order to get the highest tax value. When you file your tax return, if you pay, for example, 32% of your taxable income in taxes to the government, then on each dollar of depreciation loss applied against your income, you'll save 32 cents. In our example, there is a $3,236 tax loss. Multiply $3,236 by 32 percent: you'll save $1,035.52 in income tax. This is a return on a benefit from your investment:

$$\frac{\text{Tax Savings}}{\text{Down Payment}} = \frac{\$1,035.52}{\$10,000} = 10.3 \text{ percent}$$

A very good return on investment.

4. APPRECIATION: Appreciation is the icing on the cake in real estate investing. However, it is not possible to accurately predict the increase in future property values. Since appreciation depends heavily on inflation, supply and demand, and investor demand, you must remember that changes in appreciation rates have an effect on the rate of return from your investments. In our case, let us choose a conservative rate of 6%. Our rate of return from appreciation would be calculated by multiplying the appreciation rate of 6% by the value of $135,000, and dividing this figure by our investment of $10,000:

$$\text{Rate of increase in value X} = 6\% \times \frac{\$135,000}{\$\ 10,000} = 81\%$$

When the above rates of return are combined, you'll see your total rate of return from this real estate investment.

Cash Flow	7.2 percent
Equity Buildup	8.4 percent
Tax Savings	10.3 percent
Appreciation	81.0 percent
Cash Flow	106.9 percent

However, let's be realistic about investing in real estate. You cannot expect every property you buy to generate a return on your investment of 90% and above. You cannot expect to buy every property with a small or no down payment. My emphasis is on diligently searching for and buying property from highly motivated sellers who, for many reasons, are willing to sell their properties at a rate below market value.

To find these bargain deals, you must put in many hours of hard work, and be turned down many times, before you or anyone else can be successful. However, every rejection puts you closer to acceptance. Remember, financial independence comes with a price tag, and nothing worth anything is free.

Many experienced investors use the following formula to determine property value using the cash flow in a process called capitalization. For example, if the property in question has a net operating income (NOI) of say, $15,000, then the property value would be calculated by multiplying the net income by ten, or $15,000 x 10 = $150,000.

$$\text{Rate} = \frac{\$\,15,000}{\$150,000} = 10\%$$

Therefore, the way to determine the capitalization rate of any property is:

$$\text{Capitalization (CAP Rate)} = \frac{\text{Net Operating Income}}{\text{Price}}$$

Usually, the higher the capitalization rate, the better the investment value of the property. Therefore, if the property you are interested in buying supports a CAP rate of 11% or higher, you had better hightail it to the seller with an offer to purchase in both hands. That property can't last long on the market with such a high CAP rate.

CHAPTER THREE
GETTING SUPPORT

SELF-DISCIPLINE

Discipline is of the utmost importance in the pursuit of any endeavor. Discipline is the cover that holds the fragments together that lead to your financial goals. It does not matter what your occupation is or even if you have one, discipline is paramount. You may be highly motivated, you may feel you have everything under control, you may expect to accomplish projected goals, but you'll never reach your promised land without persistent self-discipline.

In order to experience abundance and success in your life, you must transform yourself in such a way as to be doing things according to your projected plans and strategy. According to some experts, one reason most people quit their jobs and go into business for themselves is the unwillingness to accept the discipline imposed by the corporate structure, and when they find out they must operate their own business in accordance with business rules and expectations they find themselves back where they started from, under the hammer of discipline. Self-discipline involves action; action that corrects, molds or perfects the mental faculties, giving you the ability to practice within, thus making it a means of getting support from yourself.

SUPPORT

Support is very important in the business world. Today, you need to court business activities with other agencies more than ever before. You cannot afford to be a loner. In fact, it is difficult to accomplish your goal on your own accord in the real estate market. Thus, before you set your goals, it is wise to start making connections with useful people such as a good, knowledgeable mortgage broker.

A mortgage broker will assist you with determining your qualification for various kinds of mortgages and some of the best ways to prepare yourself. Hook up with a recommended real estate agent, and locate a real estate attorney. Having expert people on your side means you'll be ready to move at full speed when you need to deal in a hurry. Also, without experts on your side, deals take longer and you'll miss details that experts would see in a split second. The mortgage market is changing as rapidly as many other sectors of the real estate industry, and technology is the driving force behind the change. Almost immediately, loan approval is possible on the web.

Therefore, be ready before you start property hunting. A lender can enter loan application information into Fannie Mae's desktop underwriter software (www.fanniemae.com) and receive a decision almost immediately. If the software determines the buyer and the property are qualified, Fannie Mae is required to purchase the loan from the originator (mortgage lender). Thus, selecting a reliable mortgage broker is very important.

HOW DO YOU CHOOSE A MORTGAGE BROKER AND ATTORNEY?
WHAT ARE GOOD QUESTIONS TO ASK?
WHAT KIND OF RESPONSES INDICATE A GOOD BROKER? ATTORNEY?

MORTGAGE BROKER

A mortgage broker is a loan provider who offers the loan product of different lenders. A mortgage broker does not lend money. Most of them are firms providing services. The mortgage broker counsels borrowers on any problem involved in qualifying for a loan, including credit problems. Brokers also help borrowers select the loan that best meets their needs, and shops for the best deal among the lenders offering that type of loan. Brokers take applications from borrowers and lock in interest rates and other terms with the lenders. They also provide borrowers with the many disclosures required by federal and state governments.

COMPILE DOCUMENTS

Brokers, in addition, compile all documents for transactions, including the credit report, property appraisal, verification of employment and assets, and so on, but not until a file is completed and handed over to the lender, who approves and funds the deal.

PAY DAY

Lenders that mortgage brokers deal with quote a "wholesale" price to the broker to get a markup in order to arrive at the "retail" price offered to the consumer. For example, the wholesale on a particular program might be 7% and zero points, to which the broker might mark up one point, resulting in an offer to that customer of 7% and one point. (Each point is equal to 1% of the loan amount, but if the broker adds a two-point markup, the customer would pay 7% and two points.)

FINDING THE BEST LOAN

The mortgage brokers' access to several loan programs of many lenders has two main advantages. First, brokers are more likely to find a loan that will meet the specialized needs of borrowers. The market is subdivided into numerous "niches," and no lender offers loans in every niche. For example, many lenders will offer loans to borrowers with poor credit, those who cannot document their income, borrowers who cannot make any down payment, borrowers who purchase a condominium as an investment, borrowers with very high existing debt, borrowers who need to close within 72 hours, or borrowers who reside abroad. The list goes on and on.

The second advantage of dealing with mortgage brokers is that the brokers are experts at jumping the market. Brokers are in a far better position that consumers to select the best deal available from competing lenders on the day terms are locked in.

DEALING WITH LENDERS ... NO GUARANTEE YOU'LL SAVE

Dealing directly with the lender could cost you more money, or you could pay less. Lenders offer "wholesale" prices to brokers because of the work brokers do for them that the lenders would otherwise have to do themselves. Lenders who operate through both wholesale and retail distribution quote wholesale prices well below retail prices.

Although there are no published statistics on wholesale/retail price differences, informed observers say that it averages about 1.5 points on a loan of $100,000.

STRENGTHEN THE APPLICATION

Not everyone who applies for a mortgage will get one. Lenders can use factors such as income, expenses, debts, and credit history to evaluate applications. You should take action to ensure that your application gets full consideration. One of the best steps is for you to give the lender or the agent all the information that supports the application.

For example, stable employment or income is important to many lenders. If you recently changed jobs, but have been employed steadily in the same field for several years, that information should be included in the application.

Before applying for a mortgage, you should get a copy of your credit report. If you have had past bill-paying problems due to a lost job or high medical expenses, you should write the lender explaining what caused the past credit problem. Lenders must consider this information upon request.

TRY FOR BEST DEAL

Some mortgage lenders may try to charge you more than others for the same loan product offered at the same time. This may include higher interest rates, origination fees or more points. You should ask the lender if the rate being quoted is the lowest offered that day. The lender is probably basing the loan offer on a rate that was issued that day to its loan officers. You should ask to see the list. If the lender refuses and you suspect that he or she is not offering you the lowest rates or points available, it may be best to look for another lender.

REJECTED APPLICATION

If your mortgage is denied, the lender must give you some specific reasons why it was denied. Under the law, you have a right to know if the application was accepted or rejected within 30 days of filing a complete application.

Know why the application was rejected. The creditor must supply a notice that tells either the specific reason for the rejection or the right to learn the reason.

Ask why you were offered less favorable terms, including higher finance charges and less money than requested.

Remember, when you need a home loan, rates are important, and the quality of service is just as important. Don't just pick a name out of a hat. Get references. Check with other investors.

SELECTING A REAL ESTATE AGENT

Select a real estate agent with good character and reputation for honest dealings and with the general knowledge of the area. Many reputable real estate agents work in areas called "farms," meaning they have designated areas where they routinely sell homes and stay current on transactions. When searching for listing agents capable of recommending the correct price for your property, stick to those who farm your neighborhood. Let the real estate agent assist you constantly in all matters, such as determining the values of properties you are interested in. Get information on the value of all listings by his or her company or other companies. Your real estate agent can be of great help to you in dealing with sellers, mortgage lenders, and buyers.

HELPING YOUR REAL ESTATE AGENT

You can help your agent big time by getting him or her referrals for sellers and buyers. Get a few of his or her cards to give out when appropriate. For instance, after you contact a FOR SALE BY OWNER and fail to get the seller to reduce his price, refer the seller to the best real estate professional in the area. Point out that he, the seller, will be much better off because the agent gets higher prices for the homes he or she sells.

As I pointed out in Chapter Nine, by performing such actions, you'll generate extra cash flow for yourself and your agent.

SHARING LISTINGS

When competition is fierce and listings get scarce, many real estate companies simply refuse to share their listings with other companies. Therefore, Realtors who do not belong to a certain group (multiple listing service) cannot automatically access information about what is on sale in that market.

Nevertheless, a good, experienced real estate agent can help you along the way, and you can, as I said before, also help the agent.

FIX CREDIT GLITCHES

Look into your credit bag before you start house hunting, and obtain full mortgage approval before looking at property. During my fifteen years as a mortgage broker, I helped many people straighten out their credit glitches. Credit deficit is a scary issue for a lot of people. However, you can correct many if not all discrepancies on a credit report.

In resolving credits snags, mortgage company representatives can be of help. Now, there's no substitute for hands-on involvement in the fix-up process. The raw data in credit reports is compiled by the three national credit bureaus: Experian, Equifax and Trans Union. Because there are often mix-ups in credit bureau reports, lenders sort through these before a mortgage can be approved.

That is why it is best to get ready and keep poised for any opportunity that pops up. You may be faced with a situation in which you run a short deadline to buy a house, or maybe you happen upon a property you think will be a good investment with excellent cash flow and sign a contract to purchase before you can get to a mortgage broker's office for mortgage approval.

No matter the reason, here are points on cleaning credit glitches:

You may have had a few credit blemishes, but your score may be on the high side. Check out a recent credit report. Federal law gives consumers free access to credit reports on a yearly basis, but some states are not yet covered. Check with your mortgage broker. You can find information on your credit rating from the Federal Trade Commission's web site, www.FTC.gov.

The Fannie Mae Foundation offers an online guide, "Knowing and Understanding Your Credit," that is available on their web site, www.Fanniemaefoundation.org.

LOOK TO YOUR MORTGAGE BROKER FOR HELP

For a quick credit fix, it is wise to head to a reliable mortgage broker for help. Scrutinize all entries on your credit report. Errors are extremely common. Search for payoff debts that are listed as unpaid, look for more than one collection for the same debt, and pinpoint any accounts that are not yours, perhaps due to a name mix-up by the credit bureaus.

I have found this to be true in several cases with clients in Detroit.

INCREASE YOUR CREDIT SCORE!

A good credit rating can help you finance and purchase a house to live in, an investment property, or expand your investment potentials. You can increase your credit score by using your credit card to establish credibility. It is a good way to build a credit rating. If you're going to buy some products or services and pay cash, use alternate credit cards instead (you should have at least three). Pay the bill in full as soon as you get it. (Get the idea?)

Increasing your credit score is a long-term process. The following are some of the most important steps to improve your credit score:

1. Pay bills on time; late payments and collections can have a serious impact on the FICO score.
2. Do not apply for credit frequently. Having a large number of inquiries shown on your credit report can lower the score.
3. Reduce credit card balances. Persons whose carry maximum balances will find their scores declining.
4. Be sure to obtain enough credit to establish a credit history. Not having sufficient credit can negatively impact the score.

LOW INTEREST RATES

I suggest you call any credit card lender who is charging you more than 9% interest and ask that your interest rate be cut. Politely explain that you'll move your balance to another card if this isn't done. Ask to speak with a supervisor if necessary. If you are refused and need to move your card balance to a lower rate card, do not close the old account. If you have property-buying plans in mind, closing consumer loan accounts can reduce your overall credit score.

GOOD CREDIT HAS ITS REWARDS

The higher your credit score, the less you'll pay for a mortgage. For example, take the cost of a $200,000, 30-year, fixed-rate mortgage. Here's a snapshot of what borrowers with varying credit scores nationwide were charged, on average, for this loan on August 5, 2005—the difference in cost between the highest credit score and the lowest score eligible for that loan is a whopping $478 a month, or $5,736 a year, which adds up to $172,221 over the life of the loan.

To find out what different loans will cost you— depending on your credit score and what state you live in—go to www.myfico.com and use the loan calculator.

Credit Score	APR	Monthly Payment	Total Interest Paid over 30 yrs.
720-850	5.793%	$1173	$222,141
700-719	5.918%	$1189	$227,888
675-699	6.456%	$1258	$253,008
620-674	7.606%	$1413	$308,671
560-619	8.531%	$1542	$355,200
500-559	9.289%	$1651	$394,362

FUTURE USE OF CREDIT SCORING

Many experts believe that residential lending will begin to use credit scoring the same way as it is used in automobile financing and consumer loans. Freddie Mac (Federal Home Loan Mortgage Corporation) is currently conducting a pilot program with large lenders. Interest rates on home mortgages may be based on the credit score. Today's 7% mortgages may be tomorrow's 6 ¾% mortgages for A+ borrowers, 7% for A, and 7¼% for B+.

UNCOLLECTED DATA

High on the list of helpful data that credit bureaus often do not collect: Consumers' utility payments for electricity, gas, water, telephone, and cable TV. Utility payments "are practically universal" and the sector is highly concentrated, so relatively few potential data furnishers would have to be convinced of the merits of reporting customer history.

Despite the complexities of coming up with fair and accurate data, several major commercial efforts are well underway. For example, at the end of April 2005, Massachusetts Statewide Housing Finance Agency began using a nontraditional credit scoring system called "anthem" that analyzes existing "thin" credit bureau data along with current and previous payments, insurance payments and child-support payments, to name a few. Changes are being made in all states to allow home lenders who truly want to provide home loans to credit worthy borrowers. Borrowers who scored poorly because they are virtually invisible to the national credit bureaus need only to give them a try.

SELL YOURSELF FIRST!

A deep-seated principle in human nature is a strong desire to be appreciated. Therefore, sell yourself first. Put shyness on the back burner and let it disintegrate. Draw others closer by extending genuine friendships and sincere interest in others, whether it comes to selling personal charm or professional ability to earn your outward attention to make other people feel special and appreciated. Such interactions will demonstrate how much you enjoy being in the presence of others and being liked by others. The normal human reaction is to like them back.

When people like you, they will support you. And what you want is support from everyone within sight or hearing. You'll cause that mortgage lender, real estate agent, buyer, seller, and others to feel good about you by helping them feel good about themselves. Sell yourself by communicating a genuine interest in others to make them feel important, valued and appreciated by impressing them as being religious, sincere, honest, down to earth, fair and straightforward.

BE PERSISTENT!

According to Edward Eggleston, "persistent people begin their success where others end in failure." You will probably find it easier if, every four or five months, you prepare a new balance sheet (assets minus liabilities equals net worth). Then you can clearly measure your progress. It also helps you to keep tabs on mistakes that may cause your progress to slow down.

When you know exactly where you stand with your capital resources, you'll be in a better position to make plans for your next move. If your resources are low, don't be dismayed. Most people are confused on the issue of capital. They think they have to have money in order to make money. Not so. You only need to know how to find money (see Chapter Six).

The most important thing to know is how to find a bargain property. Then it will be time to get concerned about taking action on the options you have in place (see Chapter Six). The motto of all creative investors should be, "if you don't have it, somebody else does." I can tell you right now that it is usually your bank. This is the essence of leverage—using other people's money!

Whatever you are doing, give it all you've got. Give every bit of yourself. Hold nothing back. Success cannot deny the person who gives life his all. Unfortunately, most people don't do this, and that is a tragic cause of failure.

A famous trapeze artist was instructing his students on how to perform on the high trapeze bar. Finally, having given them full explanations and instructions in this skill, he asked them to demonstrate their abilities.

One student looked up at the insecure perch upon which he had to perform and was suddenly filled with fear. He had a terrifying vision of himself falling to the ground. He froze completely. He couldn't move a muscle. "I can't do it. I can't do it," he gasped. The instructor put his arms around the boy's shoulders and said, "Son, you can do it, and I will tell you how." He said, "Throw your heart over the bar, and your body will follow."

Write that sentence down on the pages of your mind if you really want to do something with your life. It is packed with power.

Persistence comes from your heart. And the heart is the symbol of creative activity. Fire up the heart with where you want to go and what you want to accomplish. Be persistent.

CHAPTER FOUR
FINDING SELLERS

Having prepared yourself mentally, you're now ready to begin climbing the mountain. Your faithful real estate agent can help you in many ways. Let your real estate agent know exactly what you're doing. Let him or her know what kind of property you're looking for. Your agent will lead you to many good buys, and you can lead your agent to many good listings (houses for sale) by working together! Obviously, this is a win-win situation.

Before you begin to shop for properties, think through the type of property you would like to buy. By focusing on what you like, you'll enjoy your journey much better. Later, when you have had more experience and have acquired several properties, you may consider buying any kind of property to rent or flip. Always remember the main consideration in buying any kind of property is location, location, location!

Don't be misled by attractive prices and terms. Undesirable tenants follow undesirable locations. A drive around the neighborhood will give you the answer as to the quality of the area, whether it is improving or deteriorating. A good rule to follow in finding properties is to find the worst property in the best neighborhood at a low price. Once you locate the worst property in the best neighborhood, you'll then have a chance to upgrade the property to match existing properties in the neighborhood, and the value will increase big time!

It has been said that "you're buying the neighborhood, not just the property!" If you are doubtful about the quality of the area because there are vacant lots and some construction going on, there are people who can give you some good insight. Ask the city's planning department what is planned for the area you're considering. They will be happy to answer your questions; or you can contact a property management firm and a ask someone what's going on in the area.

As a last resort, ask the tenants (if there are any)—they usually are up to date with information on the area!

Many investors are using the internet to obtain up-to-date information on the real estate and mortgage market in preparation for finding homes to purchase and mortgage lenders to obtain financing. The internet has become the investor's primary resource for real estate and mortgage information.

RENTALS IN THE AREA

Determine if the rentals in the area are high enough to support your expected mortgage payment and still have good cash flow for your pocket. Don't assume anything here. Check it out with your faithful real estate agent. Check out nearby amenities; apartments and homes should be close to shopping centers, churches, schools and other services. If you are considering a commercial building, determine if there is adequate traffic flow before you make a commitment!

BUY THE RIGHT PROPERTY

There is more to buying property than just finding a seller. Buyers, especially beginner investors, need to ask lots of questions to avoid buying the wrong house or apartment for their situation. I have purchased rental properties where the seller's reason for selling was obvious. I still like the sellers to disclose the real reason why they are selling. Whatever the reason for selling, in many cases you can capitalize on their exit strategies. Knowing the reasons why the seller is selling puts you, as the investor, in a better position to bargain and to draw up a purchase offer to meet the seller's needs.

If you want the seller to accept your offer, try to twist things in such a way as to meet some of the sellers needs, and at the same time satisfy your own needs. Get the idea?

Try asking questions like, how much did you pay for the house? This key question (as I point out in Chapter Five) is extremely important for you and your real estate agent because it shows how much negotiation room the seller has. Related questions to ask are, what is the current mortgage balance, and are there any other liens such as a second mortgage? The answers show you how much cash the seller may need from the sale. If you learn that the seller paid a low price compared to today's market value for the property, that means the seller has lots of room to negotiate on price and terms. However, if the seller bought the property recently for only a few thousand dollars less than today's asking price, or if the property has a large mortgage with little equity, that means the seller probably won't negotiate because he needs an all-cash deal in order to satisfy the lender.

ESTATE SALE

Few people know how to locate and purchase property from an estate. Many times, the beneficiaries don't know how to market their estate; therefore, as an estate investor, you have little or no competition from other buyers. Often the property sits in limbo for months before they reach a settlement. In an estate, every type of real estate, from houses to whatever else you can think of, are in probate. Purchasing property out of an estate will assure you of a highly motivated seller. Beneficiaries are anxious to sell the property so they can pay off debts attached to the estate, such as mortgage, other creditors, or state taxes. In some situations, state assets do not need to be handled through the probate process. In many cases, you can buy property directly from the heirs or the executor of the estate.

AUCTIONS

A good way to buy property is from a foreclosure sale without actually bidding. Simply purchase the property from the winning bidder right after the foreclosure sale. Most winning bidders are buying property to flip (sell). Say someone puts in a winning bid of $150,000 on a property that has a market value of $225,000 if fixed up and with good curb appeal (looks good from the street). After the auction, offer the speculator $175,000 (or whatever). To eliminate risk, you attach several contingencies to your offer, such as permitting you to get the property inspected from top to bottom, checking out title problems, getting title insurance, and arranging financing. If negotiations work out satisfactorily, this sale closes. The speculator made a quick $25,000 (more or less), and you get the property at a good discount!

PROFIT FROM FORECLOSURE

Foreclosure property becomes available when a property owner gets in trouble and fails to fulfill his or her contractual mortgage obligations. Defaults may also occur when owners fail to pay their property taxes, or fail to pay some other related fees such as homeowner association fees, a superior mortgage claim, or special assessment.

BUY FROM A DISTRESSED OWNER

There are many ways to get foreclosure deals before the homeowner loses control and the foreclosure sale date arrives. Keep close contact with your bank. You should have at least two ways you can get good information that will lead you to good foreclosure sales. In many cases, your mortgage broker or your faithful real estate agent can point you directly to an opportunity to snag a distressed owner. You may encourage him or her to sell you the property. As the property is deeded to you, you'll become the owner.

Now you can use your brain power to negotiate a deal on the amount owed to the foreclosing lender. The lender will deal with you because you're the owner and it will not violate fair credit reporting laws.

In California, if you buy foreclosure property from someone and it is their principal residence, you must comply with California Civil Code §1695, which requires a five day right of recession and certain statutory language.

In any case, a property owner whose property is about to go into foreclosure usually will sell to the first person that comes along with money. Sometimes, property owners in foreclosure wait until the last minute before they sell to prevent their credit from going downhill.

DEALING WITH DISTRESSED OWNERS

Remember, when dealing with distressed owners do not be pushy. Be kind and understanding. Many hit the financial skids because of accidents, illnesses, business failures, divorces and many other unfortunate causes. For all these reasons and many more, they are not easy people to deal with. When you project a sense of being sensitive and understanding, and approach them with a problem-solving intent, you'll be able to reach out and help them before you help yourself. Try something new like, "Let's go to your attorney and get this monkey off your back by deeding the property to me, or a relative," and then offer to pay the attorneys fees. "If you do it now, you can stay in the house free for one month. I'll call for an appointment; where is the telephone?" Or, try some other kind of creative thinking. By now, you should have lots of options in your bag!

RUNDOWN PROPERTIES

Here's another method I have used to find bargains: While on my way to work, coming home from work, or returning home from various chores, I would take various routes throughout neighborhoods and look for run-down houses, overgrown with grass and weeds, newspapers in the yard, or no window shades up. If the property was what I would consider "rundown," I would check with the neighbors and ask if they know the owner. A good thing to tell the neighbors is that you want to get the property cleaned up. People know rundown property is bad for their property values, therefore they will be more than willing to cooperate. You may have to check public records for the name of the owner. Also try checking with the post office for a change of address form.

"SALE BY OWNER" SIGNS

I also look for "Sale By Owner" signs in sellers' yards. When I find one, I record the address on tape, with the phone number along with a brief description of the property and the nearby properties. Then I contact the owner and get information. On my initial contact, I would be extremely polite. I would give my name and the area where I live, especially if I lived in or near their area, and the church I attend. This kind of conversation relaxes a person. I would then ask about the property, how many bedrooms it has, the square footage, and asking price. Then I would ask when would be the best time to see the property. Most of the properties I acquired using this method I flipped (sold) within three months for quick profit.

ANXIOUS SELLER

The best description of an anxious seller is a person who will do most anything to dump his or her real estate. He or she may be classified as a "don't-want-to seller." He will get a personal note secured against nothing but hot air. He'll take just your signature, because he's looking for the nearest exit. This is the kind of seller all experienced real estate investors are looking for. In effect, you'll be doing a seller in this mode a favor. He wants out, you want in! What a concept!

They are praying for deliverance; you could be that deliverer. There are plenty of anxious sellers out there. In fact, ten percent of all sellers are willing to be flexible enough to be classified as anxious sellers. You still want to be sure that there are no major repairs that are needed. In most cases, it is only cosmetic, and requires no major construction.

CAN YOU FIX IT?

When you come across rundown property (and you will), don't start running in the opposite direction! It may have yellowed walls and a leaky roof. Don't be dismayed. A growing number of investors are choosing houses with room for improvement. We investors call these "fixer-uppers."

Some fixer-uppers sell for 24% less than other properties. That's the average, according to the National Association of Realtors. And get this, when they are polished up inside and out with very, very good curb appeal, they exceed the market price by 10%!

SIZE UP THE STRUCTURE!

Before you decide to make an offer, be sure to hire an inspector to doubly ensure that the house is structurally sound, and to inspect the ceiling and roof for any leaks, and the plumbing. After that, get a renovation estimate in writing. Then, add 10% to 15% for unforeseen glitches and last-minute additions to the project list.

Remember, you can save big money by using the same home repair company. Not only do I recommend you hire an engineer, I would also have a real estate attorney review the contract. There is no room to try and save money in situations like this.

NAME YOUR PRICE!

Compare three nearby homes of similar size and style that sold in that neighborhood within the last 90 days to determine the market value after renovation is complete. Factor in your time and costs, as well as the popularity of the neighborhood. You may have your faithful real estate agent get a CMA or a professional appraisal. As I said before, this is no time to try to save money!

FINDING A CONTRACTOR

If you are not connected with a building contractor, I strongly suggest that you get connected with one as soon as possible. Always have one in your bag. A good building professional can keep your renovations within firm timelines and budget. Ask for referrals from your local lumber yard. People there tend to know craftsmen on a one-to-one basis.

HANDYMAN

You also should locate a good, knowledgeable handyman. You can use him and his crew to do almost all of your work. For the most extensive jobs, use your contractor. But when it comes to ordinary detail, such as painting, carpentry, plumbing, and yard maintenance, use your handyman. Since he's an independent contractor, you'll have no liability. He has his own insurance, his own vehicle, his own equipment to work with, and his own car.

Make sure your handyman is insured. If anything goes wrong such as an accident or someone gets cheated (or thinks he did), it will be hard to sue you. It's all part of good management. You have to anticipate possible problems and stop them before they happen. By using the same handyman over and over again, you'll get the jobs done at the lowest price. I paid my handyman by the job. In all cases, he would give me a bid. If I thought I could get a lower bid, I was free to do so. But in almost all cases, I stuck with my regular handyman.

Your handyman can inspect all your properties about every six months or so. He'll observe, and then he'll come back and report to you. Is the place clean? Are the tenants changing the filters in the heater and/or in the air conditioner the way they agreed? You may not be comfortable using such tactics but they'll help you protect your assets. You'll be turning a valuable piece of property over to strangers, and you should take steps to safeguard your investment!

Your handyman can take care of small jobs when you are out of town, jobs such as leaky faucets, stopped up toilets, loose door knobs, and stopped up sinks. A handyman will do the same work as a professional for half the cost.

CHAPTER FIVE
NEGOTIATING

Negotiating is the key that unlocks the door to any successful real estate transaction, large or small, and leads to contract acceptance on all sides. This book will teach you how to negotiate better deals when you sell, rent, and buy real estate. You'll learn how to utilize enthusiasm, confidence, and secure cohesiveness with real estate agents, mortgage brokers, sellers, tenants, and your banker.

When you are a good negotiator, you'll realize that people like to deal with you. Some will recommend sellers and tenants to you. In 1969, in Detroit, a mortgage broker recommended a seller who was selling a four-unit rental property. I bought it at 25% below market value! It was one of my best investments!

ALWAYS HAVE A PLAN!

Understand that successful negotiating will result in a win-win situation for both sides, which is your first step to victory. You may not get everything you want, but you always have to be ready and willing to compromise. You may want to identify a few items you're willing to compromise on before the issue comes up. That way, you'll have a better chance of getting what's most important to you.

TIMING

I cannot stress strongly enough the importance of timing. When the seller or buyer is ready and anxious to deal, get ready. Prepare yourself, think things through. Know at what point you're willing to walk away. If you are unwilling to walk away at all, (all experts say) you're in a very weak position from the start. Knowing what your bottom line is and being willing to walk away at that point is a smart thing to be ready for.

The first benefit is your reaction. Show no emotion at all; rather, let them know your decision is what it is because it's the right business or personal decision for you. Second, having a walk-away number will give you more confidence. Lastly, it will shortcut the process. At any point, you can always ask if they will meet the price. If they say "no," the meeting can be over right then and there.

Feeling like the weaker party can certainly have an effect on the outcome of the negotiations. Always think of negotiating as a mindset rather than a skill set. Power is all in the mind, not in reality, and therefore, if you feel powerless in the relationship, then you immediately put yourself in a place of weakness during the negotiations. Level the playing field in your own mind; believe the possibilities of a successful outcome, and it's likely to happen!

WEAKNESS

Sometimes, weakness is hard to avoid and can easily create a barrier for you. However, many experts advise that you brace yourself for what could be viewed as awful, and turn it into something positive. (In other words, take a disadvantage and make an advantage out of it). That way, you put your vulnerabilities on the line so that the other person doesn't have to recount them to you.

For example, I know I don't have the $15,000 for the balance of the down payment you want, but I do have excellent credibility, and as you know, my proven management skills are outstanding. Therefore, your risk is very, very low. Such expertise will more than compensate in this situation.

YOUR STYLE

Each of us has an innate style of expression. Your style may develop to the point that people in your business circle will recognize it as yours because of your unique way of expressing yourself. The more you deal with people in the business world, the more persuasive your style will become. Donald Trump, one of New York's most powerful real estate investors, has proved this over and over and over again. By practicing using the principles in this book, you can negotiate a top deal like the pros. Accentuate sincere communication to get your way, and achieve harmony. Frank discussions may reveal a mutual admiration that leads to a beneficial meeting of the minds.

Remember, you are a part of the situation. Draw others close to you, especially in your business circles. The more you know, the more you get.

Negotiating is a vital part of the profit-making process. You should learn about the seller's financial capabilities, priorities, likes and dislikes, available options, previous offers accepted or rejected, real estate experience, his perception about the property's condition, how strong his desire to sell is, and what his needs are.

The more you know about the seller, the better you can adapt your offer and negotiating strategies to the seller's situation and personality.

You need to secure essential information and stuff it in your bag as soon as possible, while you're in the beginning stage of the negotiations. Let your perception of the seller be as realistic as your bag of information will permit. Remember, each negotiating situation is different. They all reflect a cooperative enterprise ideology, but each encounter is embodied in the seller's personality. That's why information about the seller is so vitally important.

FACE TO FACE

Always insist on negotiating directly face-to-face with the owner or decision maker, not with a representative. And don't let others negotiate on your behalf. This way you can stay close to the seller's goals. You can sense the seller's emotions ticking like a clock.

RELY ON YOUR PERSONALITY!

You need to communicate in a way that coincides with your personality. Just be yourself. Develop rapport and pick up on what the seller's needs are. This trick will gain cohesiveness with people, and they will open up to your questions.

Don't be too concerned with the condition of the property. When initially talking to the seller on the phone, you want to know whether the seller is motivated enough to make you a deal. Don't start popping tough questions that may offend the seller. Start by asking a few questions about the property, then talk about some current event that most people know about—sports and weather. Then, when the seller is responding favorably and you feel you can deal with the seller, make an appointment to see the property and negotiate!

QUESTIONS TO ASK THE SELLER

Depending on the situation, you may ask questions like: What problems have you had with the property? This open-ended question is intended to bring out hidden issues the seller may have experienced with the property. In some states, statutes and precedent court decisions don't require home sellers to disclose past problems concerning the property. But you can still ask!

What's the quality of the local schools? This question puts emphasis on the property's rental possibilities for you. If you purchase it and rent it to a family with school-age children, or if you sell it in the future, the first question prospects will ask you is, "How are the schools in the area?"

Of course, you know some of the questions, but you need to pick the seller's brain. "What's the lowest price you'll take for the property?" Or try the range technique. One of the simplest ways to gently test a seller's limits is:

Potential Buyer: *"What did you conservatively expect to get for the property?"*

Seller: *"$250,000."*

Potential Buyer: *"Really? You expect to get between $240,000 and $250,000?"*

If the seller argues, simply shrink your range until you find out how low the seller is willing to go.

This could be the last question you have. It is a good question to establish a base to work from. Regardless of what price the seller asks, it is negotiable. Armed with all the knowledge from the previous conversation, you should have a solid base to negotiate from. As a result of that conversation, you may be able to figure out the kind of need the seller has. Lean in that direction ... a little bit.

Then, according to the ongoing progress, you may come to an agreement and make out an offer to purchase, or you may suggest to the seller that you'll discuss this matter later. Sometimes it is wise to show no interest even if you can hardly wait to pop down an offer to purchase. If you opt for a later date, you'll have time to sharpen up your wits and warm up like a baseball pitcher in the bullpen.

In a case like this, if you feel good about the situation and want the property, I suggest you throw your best pitch as soon as possible.

CHECK OUT THE SELLER'S MOTIVES

In essence, try to understand why the seller is selling his property. Probably the seller hasn't been asked these kinds of questions before. Therefore, show kind, sincere and generous interest in his needs. He'll become more confident in your ability to solve his problems. As you pick deeper into the seller's brain and understand his situation, ask questions such as, if he didn't sell for several months what would happen? The answer will help you determine just how serious the seller is about wanting to sell. If he says it doesn't make any difference how long it takes, he's probably speculating and hoping someone will pay his price. If he says he must sell, he must sell before too long, before the first of the month, or in a short period of time, your seller will most likely consider creative terms.

DO YOU HAVE OTHER PROPERTIES FOR SALE?

This question might direct you to an unlisted property that may better suit your needs, or one that your real estate agent could try to list or sell. Ask the seller what he is going to do with the cash from the sale?

The seller may say he will pay off some debts. Good. This may be an opportunity to use creativity. If the conversation is going along really well, and you feel a little magnetism between you and the seller, you may feel comfortable saying, "Fine, maybe we can work something out. I'll pay that with my credit card and you can use the cash for a down payment." Sounds wacky? Well, it happens all the time, and it's far from being eccentric.

A situation like this will permit you to come up with less cash for the down payment or less cash at closing (or whatever). If the seller desires to buy a cruise ticket to Europe or whatever, offer to buy the ticket for him as a down payment on the property, but only if you can get a good deal. Find ways to uncover the real reason the seller is selling his property. You'll be in a better position to proceed with all kinds of tactics and techniques.

DECIDE WHAT PRICE AND TERMS *YOU* WANT!

Before you start negotiating, decide what price and terms you want, then move in that direction step by step. But give deep, unconditional respect to all sellers, and try to meet their needs as well as yours.

KNOW THE REAL VALUE OF THE PROPERTY

If you are buying property, it is essential that you know the approximate selling price of properties in the area. You must know that the comparative property sales in the neighborhood can determine what you should offer in your purchase contract. A good source for information is your friendly real estate agent. Ask him or her about the comparable properties that have sold in the area you are interested in. If you are not quite sure about your findings, hire an appraiser. He or she can give you a professional opinion. Use all the input you can to get a clear understanding of the true value of any property before you offer to purchase.

USE YOUR VISION

A real estate investment is a lot like being a detective. If you don't know what clues you're looking for, or where to find them, you'll have a hard time deciding whether or not to invest in a piece of property. By the time you learn the strategies in this book, you'll develop a keen set of detective's eyes, ready to spot opportunities that could lead you to a real estate gold mine! Look for undiscovered potential for adding value to the property. See Chapter Eight.

ALWAYS REMEMBER: THE FIRST TO MENTION NUMBERS, LOSES

If you wait long enough, the seller will reveal where he will go regarding the price. Don't mention any numbers. If you do, you may weaken your position. The conversation may go something like this:

Seller: *"I've got to have $60,000 or I won't sell."*

Silence.

Seller: *"Because that's the figure I said I needed."*

Silence.

Seller: **"Well, I guess I could settle for $55,000 if you pay all the closing costs."**

Silence.

Seller: *"I won't sell for a penny below $53,000."*

Let the seller do the talking. Silence is devastating if used in the right place at the right time. As soon as you have all the information you need, go somewhere and analyze all the data that you have collected, and prepare a formal offer to purchase. Keep a positive attitude and court the situation at hand. Draw upon the negotiating knowledge you have learned, and construct an offer to purchase accordingly.

TIME IS OF THE ESSENCE

If you're going to meet the owner to negotiate some kind of deal, don't fritter away valuable time. The more organized you are, the further ahead you'll be at the negotiating table. Speak to some of his tenants a day or so before the meeting, ask what they think about the landlord. Check out the property to see the condition. Get all the information that will give you negotiating power and room to wriggle (negotiate).

Just because someone is much more successful than you, owns a lot of property, holds a high-end position at a company, the bottom line is, it makes no difference. You can still relate to each other big time. Leave negativity in the garbage can at home and head for the negotiating table.

Negotiate directly with the seller face to face. If the seller is firm with his price, you must be able to negotiate flexible terms. If the seller is firm on his terms, you must be able to choose the price (usually lower). Whenever possible, try to choose both the price and the terms. Then, if you're not successful achieving your price and your terms, move on. Remember, there are twenty more properties just around the corner on Sycamore Street!

Destroy the expectations of high profit in the seller's mind. Pop holes in the seller's desire for a high price. Don't be thrown by the seller's fancy reasons why his property is worth more than anyone else's property in the area, even if it is on Sycamore Street! Go over the property very carefully and observe every negative thing about it!

You do this for a good reason ... you may not want the property after all. You want to show the seller his property has flaws and needs correcting. This will help later on if you desire to require the seller to correct all of the flaws you found in your inspection before you buy his property, or if you have already decided to buy it, act interested in the seller's property.

Don't forget to let the seller know that you are ready to buy, **but** this property is just one of several you'll see that day. And strongly indicate that there are competitive properties on the market. Show the seller figures on comparable properties. Do this with a down-to-earth, friendly attitude, but be firm. The more you learn about the property in question and the situation, the more useful the information you will bring to the negotiating table!

GET THE BEST TERMS!

Buy property at the lowest price possible and negotiate for the best terms! Never accept concession without receiving something in return. This strategy is used more and more by real estate investors. Big dealers and small dealers alike use it all the time. If the seller asks for more money down, you ask for more time. If the seller asks for a higher price, you ask for less money down. A check list can also be a good negotiating tool. A seller has no ground to stand on when you present him or her with a detailed list of the faults. Each item on the list is worth money to you. Each fault means more room for one more concession the seller has to deal with in order to proceed with the deal. You might get the price lower, or get better terms. In any case, you should get something!

Use good negotiating skills and put them to work for you. Go after the investment you crave, but only if wisely planned. Then, add a steady hand to the helm, and guide yourself to the promised land.

Remember, hidden negative desires may rise to the surface of your mind. But don't take off on a poorly planned expedition to pan for gold when a gold mine is in your own backyard!

CHAPTER SIX
FUNDING

Acquiring loans to purchase property is easier than most people think. Many beginners in real estate investing are simply afraid to make offers to buy property because they are not sure how they will get the money needed to purchase. Don't worry, have faith; money is all around you!

GET READY

List all your assets (if you have any). List all your liabilities. Then subtract your liabilities from your assets.

Now you have a good idea of your total net worth. If you have nothing (like many millionaires started with), fear not! You have the best asset in the world—your brain!

Now you can start getting ready for your first real estate investment. Don't wait until you need money. Believe it or not, when you don't need money is when the banks are more inclined to give you a loan! Remember, you are not only investing in real estate, you are investing in yourself! Don't despair if your budget is as tight as fiddle strings. You can push forward by using principles outlined in this book.

STRONG FINANCIAL POSITION

When your financial position is strong, the bank's risk is low, making you an ideal borrower. They usually ask you why you need a loan? Then they reach their own assessments of the reason you need the money. Learn more about this so you'll be in a better position to handle yourself when borrowing money from banks.

Don't let bankers make decisions for you. Their business is lending money, not making real estate deals. You make the deals ... they lend the money. Remember, when dealing with any lending institution, make sure you project your good personal qualities that inspire confidence! You will find immediately that they want to help you or even just see things your way. Show them qualities like enthusiasm, preparation, showmanship and tenacity!

ESTABLISH CREDIT

Here is a simple method that many investors use to establish powerful credit with lending institutions: make a financial statement and always have it ready. Visit your bank and ask to borrow $4,000 (more or less depending on your financial status). When they ask you the reason for the loan, tell them you are a real estate investor and you want to position yourself to make an investment when an opportunity presents itself. If they ask you for your financial statement, give it to them.

Be sure it shows your assets that can be converted to cash, such as stocks, bonds, surrender value of insurance policies, or anything else of value. Offer it as security for the loan. Remember, this action is simply to establish credit. You have the right to pay the loan any time without penalty.

PAY BACK THE LOAN

Pay off the loan using the same money you borrowed. Then, return to the same bank and borrow $10,000 (more or less) and again pay back ahead of time. Establish a perfect payment record with your bank. If you put the money in another account that earns interest, all you'll lose is the difference in the interest rate you pay the bank and the interest rate you earned on the money you put in the bank.

At this point in time, you may consider using the borrowed money to pay down on a piece of rental property with a good net operating income (NOI). The property will pay back the loan, and you can reinvest the NOI.

REDUCE SECURITY RISK

As you begin to feel more comfortable along the way, ask your bank to return or reduce your security based on your actual credit record. If they refuse, simply tell them you're thinking of taking your account to another bank that is more flexible.

If the loan officer still refuses, ask to talk to a supervisor who will probably be more receptive to your wishes. What you're doing is establishing good relationships with the bank. You want bankers to know you and trust your judgment. They will love you! When you really need a loan, the bank will be there to assist you with your investments. Keep in mind that banks don't like to lose business from good customers!

HARD MONEY LENDERS

There are some institutions that you may consider hard money lenders. These are commercial banks, thrift institutions, finance companies, credit unions, and cash-by-mail companies, to name a few. They all have their particular lending guidelines, and each has different goals and objectives.

However, you can handle them with good credit. As you gain confidence and experience, you'll find out which lending institution you like to deal with.

USE SEVERAL BANKS

At a minimum, use two banks. Deposit your money into as many banks as you feel is right for you. You will find that your borrowing power will multiply. It may take time to establish a strong relationship with some banks, but believe me, it's worth the wait, it is necessary, and most importantly, it works!

Banks are in a highly competitive business, so don't be afraid to get up, shake hands, and walk out of a bank that is not responsive to your needs and wishes! As soon as you leave that bank, go straight to another one! When you get strong capital, go back to the bank that turned you down and get more than you want! Get what I mean?

KNOW THE MANAGER

Get to know the manager of the bank where you do business. You'll soon realize that the bank officers and lending institution personnel are ordinary, friendly people (just as friendly as you are). The more you know about borrowing, the more courage and confidence you'll have in your ability to handle any financial situation. The fat-cats may now borrow money in the millions, but when they started, they just borrowed whatever little they could get.

HOW MUCH MONEY DO YOU NEED?

How much money do you need to get started? I'll say loud and clear—$0! All you need is knowledge of how to get money. Borrowing money is like borrowing tools to work with. When you finish with the tool, you return it to its owner. But look at how much you have accomplished by using other people's tools (you may even let someone else return the tool for you, like the cash flow from tenants on Sycamore Street). Get what I mean?

HOMEOWNER

If you're a homeowner and your obvious money source is your home equity—four walls and a small fortune—consider getting a second mortgage. Stash the money in the bank so that it will be ready to be used as a down payment on investment property! Let someone else pay it back (the tenants). Before you use the money, remember, *Them that got ... GETS!*

Here's an example: If you have $8,000 dollars in savings, there is little hassle in borrowing another $8,000. The lending institution will probably require holding your account as collateral. But now you have $8,000 of other people's money (OPM) plus the original $8,000 (less the amount of interest on that debt of course). If you reverse the process by spending the $8,000 and then try to borrow that amount again, you will have about as much chance for success as that guy who went bear hunting with a switch!

DIFFERENT LEVELS

Remember, there are different levels of bank officers. While a regular loan officer at a branch may have a loan authorizing limit of $10,000, a senior loan officer at the main location can go much higher without requiring committee approval.

CREATIVITY

You can buy real estate with little or no money down! This does not mean that the seller, in many cases, receives no down payment. What happens in those cases is how the money for the down payment came out of someone else's pocket, not yours!

Creativity is of the utmost importance. Try your hardest to practice creative solutions, and whenever you can, deal with people who are creative. Look for solutions other than cash to satisfy the deal. Some people, including some real estate agents, will tell you that the only road to successful real estate investing is paved with cash.

BULL!

Don't ever believe such a misconception. An investor can run out of cash. He'll never run out of creativity. Cash loses value, creativity never loses value. In gaining prosperity with little or no money down, creativity is your most vital asset!

LITTLE OR NO CASH DOWN

Take your creativity and combine it with visualization, and your mind begins to formulate solutions that will help you acquire property with little or no money down!

For example, I learned from an associate that a friend of his wanted to sell his house. He told me a great deal about the seller. The seller did not want to fix up his property. He had no mortgage on the property and he had been trying to sell his property for three months. On the next day, I made an appointment with the seller to see the property. As I approached the house, I knew right away why it hadn't sold. The property was in poor condition.

I entered the house and met the seller. I began talking about the lovely tropical trees in the area. The seller seemed to be getting comfortable. I then asked to see the house. I was more than a little surprised that the interior was in good condition. The basement was ideal for an apartment, and it had its own entrance and exit. I remember saying to myself, "Wow! Bird nests on the ground!" I decided right then and there that I wanted the property if a deal could be reached. After the seller was comfortable with me, I began to dig to find out his exit strategies and why.

I asked him why he was selling. He said he wanted to live in a community where his friend was living because he was tired of keeping up the property. I asked him if I bought the property what he and his wife would do with the money. They smiled, and he said softly, "pay rent." Then I said that was a "good idea." I knew I had to sell myself right then and there or come back another day. I put my hand on his shoulder and said loud and clear, "I have a good plan for you! Let me give you some people as references so you and your wife will know me better." I really wanted them to trust me.

I gave them my two bank managers' cards, my real estate agent's card, my loan officer's card, and also my card. I said that if they had any doubts about my character, to please call these people and ask about me.

Then I asked the big question, *"How much are you asking for the property?"*

"$85,000," he replied.

"In this condition?" I asked.

"Yep," he replied.

I knew that a three-unit house was worth his asking price, and the reason he hadn't sold it was because it had zero curb appeal! From the street it looked "sick." I said, as we sat at the dining room table, "Here is my plan. I'm sure it will work for you, but first, let me go over some facts with you. If you sell this property, you will have to make the property attractive. Is that right?"

"Yes."

"Not only for potential buyers, but for the mortgage company. And if you sell, you'll have the money in the bank earning very little interest. While, if I buy your property, you'll sell without making any repairs and get a high interest rate. And you'll still have the deed in your name until the house is paid for!"

We discussed price and terms over and over again. Finally, we agreed on a price of $84,000 at 7% interest, and a $3,000 credit for repairs as a down payment. I made out a purchase agreement and a loan contract for $81,000 at 7% for twenty-one years. As I recall, the deal closed in approximately six days.

No money came out of my pocket for this deal! All cleanup and repair costs came from rental income.

RENTAL INCOME

Upper 2/1	$650
Up 1/1	$550
First floor 3/2	$840
Basement 1/1	$500
	$2,540
NOTE:	$ -995
	$1,545

Tax & Ins.	$ -198
	$1,344
Utilities	$ -350

CASH FLOW   ***$997***

A loan contract in some states is referred to as a contract for deed, contract for sale, or agreement of sale, and permits buyers to pay sellers for the property in installments. The buyer agrees to buy a property and pay principle and interest to the seller. Unlike mortgage financing, most often title to the property remains in the seller's name until all agreements in the contract are fulfilled. As you can see, savvy creative financing is not just for savvy investors. It works for savvy sellers as well.

STICK WITH THE NORM

Do remember that there are a few properties you come across that require little or no down payment. I strongly suggest to any beginner to prepare yourself to purchase your first property according to the norm with regular qualifying and regular down payment. I purchased eighteen properties in three years. Only three were zero down deals, and four were with low down payments. The rest were according to the norm. A good trick that works is to buy properties you can fix up, add on, so that you can increase that cash flow coming in wave after wave after wave!

Some experts call this fixing up or improving the real estate "forced inflation," because the property increases in rental value after improvements have been made.

For example, install new carpets using your handyman to do the work; paint interiors, install drapes and curtains. Improve the exterior if it needs to be made more attractive; this is where you should actually start improving the property.

These improvements will give you an opportunity to increase the rents. Thus, forced inflation is in place.

CHAPTER SEVEN
TENANTS

It has been said, "Getting tenants is like going fishing. You can't go fishing without the right bait." The right bait to attract the right kind of tenant you want is the right kind of property. Remember this principle, everyone wants to step up in the world, not down. Therefore, you should buy property with the future tenants in mind. You want your future tenants to think of your property as their home.

ADVERTISING

Getting tenants is easy. Getting the right kind of tenants takes planning, judgment of character, and experience.

There are many different media: TV, radio, newspaper and others. No matter what you pick, you've got to let people know you're there. Some landlords simply put a sign in the window or in front of the building. The sign should be large enough so you can put large bold letters "RENT" or "TO LET" with a small phone number under the main word.

The sign should be large enough so it can be seen by people passing in cars. The small sign in the window will only cover the neighbors and people who will pass the information on to others. If there is a big demand for rentals, very little advertising is required. In many cases, you will have a list of people waiting to get an apartment. Therefore, it is just a matter of phoning those on the list.

NEWSPAPER

In most cases, it is wise to start your ad one month before you have a vacancy. This way you'll have less of a chance of losing money from vacant units. Remember, you are selling time! If you have a unit vacant for any amount of time, you can never recover the time. It is unlike retail business, where if you don't sell a color TV today, you sell it next week, so what!

Many beginner investors make the mistake of letting units stay vacant before they get them cleaned up and rented. Your ad should state the general area and north or south of the main street. In a large city, the street only can be used. Look at ads in the newspaper and follow them as a guide, making adjustments to fit your needs! Always play up the attractive aspects such as: close to transportation, near shopping, or seven minutes to the airport, etc.

PROPERTY ADDRESS

Do not put the rental property's address in the ad—people will go directly to the property without an appointment. Therefore, you want to have an opportunity to interview them and ask them information such as: what's your occupation, or how many people are there in your family? Sometimes people want to move into a one-bedroom unit with their mother, father and three children. In the first phone call, you can tell them it cannot be done. Also, some people will neglect to control their children by letting them run wild without supervision, or they can just be obnoxious once they decide they don't want the place. Most newspapers offer ad space for two, three or four-line minimums for a flat fee. Check your newspaper for details. A four-line ad costs more than a two-line ad, but it is twice as effective.

MILITARY NEWSPAPERS

If you live near a military base, the military newspaper is a good place to advertise. Military people make excellent tenants because they know how to follow rules and they have steady employment. You can use various methods. It depends on your situation, the size of your operation, the nature of the rental market in your area, and your own personality.

GETTING CALLS

Now that your ad is in place, put a pencil and notebook by the phone. Write down details about the ad so that other people answering your phone will know what the ad says, and therefore can handle the situation more intelligently. You may sit around the phone and take down the names and phone numbers of the callers your ad has attracted. When you call them back, engage them in a pleasant conversation. Let them know you would like to have them as tenants. But while interviewing them, definitely ask the right questions so you can then determine whether you want to show them the property. If people turn you down because they feel your rental price is too high, it will be wise to give your price some reconsideration, as you really might be too high. Do your homework. Make sure your rental rates are close to the going rates in the area, and then don't back down without a concession of some kind. However, your rates may be just a little on the high side. This will give you room to drop them down just a little. While you have them on the phone, find out if they're the kind of people you want. Tell them a little bit about your program and what you expect from your tenants, such as discount programs, finder's fee, and tenants taking part in constructing the lease or rental agreement. This idea will go over big time with the caller.

FINDER'S FEE

If you're renting an apartment, you may consider a tactic many landlords use. Give a finder's fee of $50 to the tenants already in the other apartments. This helps both you and the tenants, because they will be living close to people they know, and usually, they will be better tenants in following the rules and expectations of the community.

APPLICATION FORMS

Get application forms ready. You may get some from your faithful real estate agent whom you are closely in touch with, or go to the nearest office supply store. For a large size operation, you can have them printed to order. Information in the application is necessary to start a file on the person, mainly for identification. Assure the applicant that you will check their credit and references. The information in the application helps to determine how stable they are, how long they have worked on their job, and how long they have lived at their present address.

Have them sign the application or sign some kind of document giving you permission to check their credit. Action on the application should be completed within 24 hours.

DEPOSIT

Request a deposit of $100. This will determine if the prospective tenant keeps cash, but if they don't have that much, accept less, with the remainder due on the receipt as additional deposit due at a specific time and date. Always accept cash instead of checks. People will put checks for deposits on more than one rental in order to hold them while making up their minds about another house or apartment. A service fee is sometimes charged to check credit, draw up a lease, and set up the file.

Be sure to explain all of this in detail.

RETURN DEPOSIT

If the tenant does not pass the credit check, when the lease is made out and ready to be signed, return the full deposit at once. Get a receipt for the returned deposit so you will have a record. No money can be kept on a rental deposit unless the renter moves in or a lease is signed. Explain to the prospective tenant why you turned him or her down. Show them the report.

CREDIT CHECK

If the credit check and references indicate the tenant is a poor risk, do not take any chance renting to him or her. Wait for someone else even at the risk of reducing rent. A credit check should be made, and if you do not belong to a credit bureau, ask your faithful real state agent to do it for you. Know who will do your credit checking before you advertise for tenants. Be ready!

All of this information depends on the time you have and the market conditions.

HOLDING A PLACE

Never hold a place for a person unless the lease is signed, and do not stop advertising, taking applications or deposits until a lease is actually signed. Remember, deposits and applications mean little. Signing of the lease constitutes releasing the property to the prospect. When he or she moves in is his or her business. Also, after the lease has been signed and money has been paid, then hand over the keys and get a receipt for the keys.

SECURITY DEPOSIT

A security deposit is mandatory on all rental contracts. It is described in full detail as a security or damage deposit, and under no circumstances will it be used for the last month's rent. The security deposit is usually the same as a month's rent or what you feel is adequate for your particular situation. If you find a tenant's application is doubtful, then double the security deposit. For example, if his references or credit report shows that he has always worked, but never held a steady job and has poor credit, but he wants to rent the apartment for $300 per month, then set the deposit at $600 so that it will cost him a fee of $900 to move in.

It's a good idea to remember your tenants and handyman with Christmas cards. This interaction promotes a feeling of appreciation and that you are not too far from them should they need you.

RETURN SECURITY DEPOSIT

Always set a date three or four days after a tenant vacates the property to return a security deposit. Make your inspection immediately after the tenant leaves. In some cases, conduct the inspection the last few minutes while they are still on the premises. The premises should be cleaned up and no furniture or any items left behind. Follow the checklist signed with the lease or rental agreement.

Always check everything very closely. Run your hands over the countertop edges, bathroom fixtures and sinks. Describe all the damage you find in detail.

If everything is okay, you may consider making out a check for the security deposit, and hand it over to the tenant with a smile on your face. After all, the tenant has participated in paying the note on the property for you.

INSPECTION KIT

A good inspection kit is made up of paper and pencil, checklist, flashlight, yardstick, and light bulbs. Turn on all lights and replace any that are burned out. Then, start at the front door. Move right or left all around the house or apartment. Check every window to see if any are broken, check all handles to see if they are loose, or walls to see if they are marked up.

Try all moving items such as the kitchen drawers and doors. Check bath tile for breaks and scratches. Check bath fixtures, flush toilets, and check the furnace filter. Many times, you just take the filter out and throw it away. Remember, filters should be kept clean or the back pressure caused by dust and dirt will make the fan motor burn up.

Some tenants will leave the premises in excellent condition and pass with flying colors. You should refund the money to these people immediately. To the others with damaged property, make up a bill and get a licensed contractor to repair damage as soon as possible. Subtract the cost of the repairs from this list, explain the repairs, and talk it over with the tenant. Keep the repair costs as low as possible. Send the balance of the security deposit to the tenant, with receipts for repairs.

PICTURES

Be sure to take pictures of all major damage and have a witness, a neighbor or a friend with you. If there is a real serious damage situation, get a police report to help substantiate the extent of the damage. Use a yardstick to show the size of the gadgets or broken wall sections, especially when held over the damaged area and photographed. If the cost of the damage is more than the security deposit, bill the tenant for the difference.

COLLECTING

Have all the tenants pay rent with a check or money order. This way you can keep records and avoid the risky problem of handling cash. You may consider getting a post office box. This way, your home address will be private.

CHOOSE THE RIGHT TENANT

Choosing the right tenant is important to you and the tenant. Interview prospective tenants on the phone, as I advised you, before you meet them face to face. You can find out if they are the kind of people you most likely want, and they can find out if the property is right for them. You can tell them about your rental program and what you expect from your tenants. Tell them about your discount program (if you have one). It's good to have one for taking care of the minor maintenance, and giving discounts for paying rent on time. This discount idea is a good deal for the tenant who intends to make payments on time and follow the rules outlined in the contract. Dig deep and ask as many questions as you can, and be sure to answer all of their questions.

If they don't sound right, end the discussion. I firmly believe it is up to you to pick your tenant rather than letting your tenant pick you.

MEETING THE TENANTS

Have all your paperwork in place. All favorable prospects must fill out an application and then be interviewed. During the interview, pick the applicants' brain and dig deep. Observe their body language. You might ask them, "Please fill out this form so I can check your personal references and check your credit." If the applicants show signs of being uncomfortable, take a deeper look. They may give you reasons to reject them right then and there. I remember asking them right out to tell me about the bad part that they are uncomfortable about. Look them straight in the eyes and have them spit it out. (Thanks to a few hours of psychology I had in college).

Some experts say that you should never meet your prospective tenants at the rental property. Meet them in your office or someplace else. From my experience I say, meet them at the rental property with their entire family. You'll have a chance to observe them face to face as they view the property and answer questions, and always ask lots of questions. You'll get a deeper feeling about their personality and their character. When you meet prospective tenants on the premises, you get to know them better.

CREDIT CHECK

If they like the property and want to rent it, have them fill out a credit application and pay you a credit check fee before proceeding any further.

Credit checks will tell you a lot about people. Time and time again, I found that people who give you a long, tall story are usually lying. They are hoping you'll feel sorry for them. You must stand firm. You are not acting as a social worker. However, be polite and understanding. Give them kindness and deep respect.

When checking their personal references, pay little attention to what their previous landlords may have said. They may want to get rid of them. Pay little or no attention to mom and dad; they think their sons or daughters are angels even if they don't have wings.

Rely on the credit report and similar information. Job references are usually good.

BODY LANGUAGE

Notice their body language; it will point your mind toward the realization of their inner selves. You may not be a psychologist, but you're not a fool either. Use your common sense.

Remember, you are setting up a business and you must put God first and your business second. Keep people problems out of this scenario. Not even your own problems should distract you from focusing on your goals. Don't cave in, crumble, or fall apart.

Smart cookies don't crumble!

CHAPTER EIGHT
RENTAL INCOME

The most prosperous people under the sun are involved one way or another in land called real estate. Large owners are called landlords or landladies. Rental property is a fantastic investment. Income will start buzzing when you get your first tenant. According to experts, a good income-producing property is the safest investment you can own.

Once you close a deal and take title, it becomes your money tree. Cash flow depends on how much service you provide and how much you develop it. Mike Gifford says, the more you care, the more you provide, the more fruit it will produce.

Well-kept property, as pointed out in Chapter Eleven, will provide a great return on your investment, money and time, wave after wave after wave, which will then compound your investment dollars over and over and over again.

STOCKS AND BONDS

When other investments such as stocks and bonds fade away, real estate will be left standing taller than ever. When stocks fall flat on the bottom plank on the floor, many stock investors reach out with a trembling arm and grab for a savior ... usually real estate, or God!

You might say owning real estate is more than just a home, it's where life will blossom.

SETTING THE RENTAL PRICE

Check comparable rental properties to determine what the average property is renting for. Some landlords believe that by keeping rents low the tenants will not move out and they will have nice tenants.

Experience has shown time and time again, and experts agree, that this is a misconception.

Value is the norm today. Rents scales vary enormously in some areas, from well-kept, sharp buildings to run-down tenements. The most rent-able units seem to be in the middle-priced range. Try offering many different apartments with many different styles in the same building—one bedroom, two bedroom and three bedrooms that are priced accordingly.

In a tight rental market, single family home rentals will be booming. They will rent for more than luxury apartments.

In any case, check out the rental rates for the kind of property you are dealing with in your area. Be very discreet in setting rental prices. If you are renting an apartment, you may decide not to take children or pets. But both are usually welcome in the single family home or duplex (two family home).

In a single family home, the tenants are often required to mow the lawn, shovel the snow, and keep up the outside appearances of the grounds. In exchange for this work, the tenant has privacy, and may have children and pets, and engage in activities that renters in apartments cannot.

Set your rent a little higher than the going rates. If you set your rates a little higher, you can always come down. It is difficult to go up once the price is announced. Be sure you check very close on the going rates in the community, and don't let the applicant know more than you about this.

Setting the rental rates of one apartment complex does not present a problem like single family or duplex homes do.

DISCOUNTS

Setting your rent slightly higher and giving a discount for rent paid on time is a good way to encourage tenants to pay rent on time. For instance, if the average rent for a single unit is $850, you rent it for $900. But if paid on or before time, it is $825.

MAILING ADDRESS

You may consider getting a post office box so tenants can mail their rent payments to your post office box instead of your home. If possible, you may get tenants to open accounts at your bank. This way, each month you can have the money automatically transferred from their accounts to yours. In most cases, the bank will give you points for bringing in new customers. This will also go over big time with your bank manager. He will be more favorable to you when you apply for that next loan. Get the point?

You may give your tenants twelve self-addressed envelopes. This will encourage the tenants to act.

ESTABLISH A BUSINESS ADDRESS

After you become established—say you own three rental properties—you may consider establishing a company or corporation. I established a business called Goodyear Development Company, with a post office box number. I was the president. Stanley Goldstein was the fake name I gave to the tenants as the owner. Whenever I confronted tenants, I announced myself as a part-time employee for the company and also a tenant.

In several cases since, I had conflicts with tenants. They wanted to speak with the owner. The owner was always out of town. (Get the idea?) This was one of the best tricks I had in my bag.

I conducted all of my business under my company name. My company had its own checking account. This also went over big with my bank manager.

INCREASE CASH FLOW

When buying property, use your vision and look for room to wriggle. Search out ways you can develop the property to its highest and best use to increase cash flow. Before you buy property, especially single family houses, check to see if you can renovate the property by adding on rooms or any other conversions you may have in mind. Check and see what other investors are doing in your area and different areas within the same county, and what their policies are. Be like the pros. Think creatively about the ways to get the highest and best use from a property before you buy it. This is a concept known well in the real estate industry.

CASH FLOW FROM RENOVATIONS

Let's look at a possibility that's very good for a beginner real estate investor. This idea is good even if you do it in your own home…

Most garages are scary places, to put it mildly. A state of chaos remains even after it has been so called "cleaned up." Monstrous lawn mowers and leaf blowers lurk in the shadows. Garden hoses and electrical cords lie in wild knots. Tennis balls are scattered throughout. Get rid of this stuff. Go buy a metal ten-by-ten shed (or whatever) to store this stuff in, then convert the garage into a one-bedroom, one-bath unit. This tactic is especially good for the beginner investor because it increases cash flow that can be reinvested in other properties. For example, in most areas of the country, a one-bedroom apartment rents for $600 a month, or $7,200 a year, less the cost of renovating it.

Check out and see what other people are doing in the area to get an income increased from their properties. There are always more ways than one to skin a cat!

LEASE

All leases are not the same. Some embody clauses that you may think only cause instability. Be sure to have your lease reflect your needs in fulfilling your purpose. See your real estate agent. He or she may have a lease you can use as a guide.

TENANT TAKES PART IN PREPARING THE LEASE

I found this to be very helpful in getting the tenants' cooperation in keeping up with what tenants are expected to do. But when filling out the lease, permit the prospective tenant to make some decision in its construction. People feel more committed to agreements when they take part in shaping them.

The idea is to project cohesion and adjust the lease to fit your needs and the needs of the tenant. For example, you would tell your tenant, "Your rent is $975 per month. What would you prefer, you cutting the grass and paying $925 a month, or paying $975 a month and having your landlord getting the grass cut?"

A well-oiled, smooth-running machine is what you'll end up with, and with the right incentives, a cooperative tenant will end up with a caring, understanding landlord!

Remember, all your ideas will not come to you as sudden inspirations or revelations. You'll find that experience, especially working with tenants and sellers, will shed light in many dark corners of your mind, and lead you to your gold!

Your prospective tenant may join you in drawing up the lease, but be sure to go over the agreement word by word, line by line. Make sure the applicant understands the agreement in its entirety before he or she signs it.

PREVENTING PROBLEMS

A well-constructed lease may help prevent problems because you and the tenant know what is expected of each of you. Check your properties or have your handyman check in on the properties periodically. In this way, you will stop problems before they start. Make repairs as soon as possible. This way the costs will be much less, and therefore you'll keep your maintenance costs down.

In other words, just keep up the property. Fix little repairs before things fall apart and become a problem! Not only is it wise to fix little things to keep the property in tip-top physical condition, but conducting creative and appealing improvements always adds the most value.

Teach your handyman to look for possible defects when doing routine chores. For instance, your handyman may be routinely checking air-conditioning filters. However, he can also keep an eye out for loose door knobs, cracked window panes, leaky faucets, trash in the yard, mold in the bathroom, or any other potential problems.

CHAPTER NINE
RENT OR SELL

Most savvy real estate investors seldom see his or her investment properties as poor income producing cows. But if you come across a very good bargain such as a large apartment building with good cash flow that will significantly enhance your financial position, you may consider selling all or a part of your properties. You'll be moving up to a larger apartment building, consolidating your diverse equities, and increasing your borrowing power. Your management responsibility will be centered in one location, giving you better control. Your cash flow will increase, giving you more leverage to push forward with your increased buying power!

BUY LOW, SELL HIGH

You can buy choice real estate big time 10% to 15% below market value, even well below market value, and earn thousands of dollars on each transaction, or you may opt to hold onto and rent the property. In any case, you should have a plan for each deal you make, a plan as to how you'll handle the situation, rent or sell. If you rent it, you'll soon recover your down payment. You can reinvest the same money in another property and have the first property free, with cash flow corning in wave after wave after wave. You can you do this with single family homes, duplex units, apartments, or any kind of property.

You can find profit-making opportunity in every neighborhood. Approximately 10% of all properties for sale are selling below market value, making it possible for a beginner investor to move ahead, slowly but surely. Once real estate investors reach a firm financial footing, they might choose properties that are selling 15% to 20% below market value in a good neighborhood. Give the property a smiling facelift and then sell or rent it at its highest market value.

Remember, no matter how much time and money you put into your property to improve it, the location will have a profound effect on the amount of rent you can receive from any property. That's why it is so important to analyze your situation carefully without your checkbook in your hand.

You can knock out walls and make rooms larger, repair the heating, add on a new bathroom, convert a garage to a rental unit, and much more, but you can never upgrade an undesirable neighborhood.

REAL ESTATE AGENT

Real estate agents are essential when choosing people to have on your team. But you should explain to them how you work and your investment practices.

Real estate agents prefer home buyers with cash for down payments, good income, good credit rating. Their vision is getting the job done with as little work as possible. They are not up to understanding creativity in pushing deals forward. They're not very receptive to unusual offers. Without their knowing how you work, if you hand an agent an offer to purchase a property with no down payment, he'll look at you and say *"So you think I'm stupid?"*

They will think you are not serious about buying. They simply do not like creative offers. They like conventional offers from the regular buying public. Investors tend to throw too many curveballs. However, once the agent tunes in on your wavelengths, you'll find that working together will be very profitable on both sides.

Working hand in hand all the time with one or two particular agents who are in tune with your moves, twists and turns, and the curveballs you throw, you and the agent can do great things working together as a team, and you can help each other big time as I said! It is very important to hook up with a good, experienced real estate agent or broker. The bottom line is to position yourself in an environment that will open doors for you to better generate cash flow. In any case, that requires negotiating, and two heads are always better than one.

OPPORTUNITY

You may consider selling some or all of your properties. It depends on many factors. For instance, if you come across an opportunity to buy an attractive apartment building and you are very sure it is an excellent investment that will significantly enhance your financial position and your cash flow, you might consider selling part or all of your properties. You'll be taking a big step forward. You'll be acquiring property that will allow you to consolidate and increase your cash flow, which will increase your borrowing power, which will increase your leverage.

You will take title to the apartment building, and your management duties will be centered in one location. You'll have better control and annual tax deductions for your property's depreciation. See Chapter Two.

ACCEPT EQUITIES

Sometimes a seller will accept your property in exchange for down payment on his property. Your property might be just what he or she is looking for. On the other hand, the seller might insist on cash because he is doing just what you're doing, moving up to a bigger and better property.

If you are serious about buying the property, tie up his property with a well-written contract and a contingency clause that states the contract is subject to the sale of your property. Tell your faithful real estate agent exactly what you are doing.

CURB APPEAL

If you are selling or renting property, always pay close attention to curb appeal. Curb appeal is very important in attracting would-be buyers or tenants.

The main thing is to accentuate whatever is positive about the property's good features. You can start by taking a good hard look at it and not through the swift, forgiving glances you usually give it as you enter and leave. Give it a longer, dispassionate, critical gaze from a distance. Walk across the street and see the property through a stranger's eyes. Is there anything that just doesn't look right? Old, worn-out screens, bad-looking shutters, a sad, beat-up front door? Get rid of them and replace them with fresh, good-looking ones.

Rarely does a home sell on advertising alone. Creating effective marketing materials can help draw prospective buyers and renters to a property they might be unwilling to visit due to its lack of curb appeal. What are some of the strong points that often influence buyers or renters? Maybe you have a great floor plan, wonderful natural light, a desirable location, or excellent schools. Try to remember the factors that drew you to the property when you bought it.

Make sure your listing agent includes several positives about your property in its Multiple Listing Service entry, as well as in ads and marketing brochures. Ask your faithful real estate agent to stage one or more broker's opens (open houses). Most people are familiar with public open houses where anyone can show up, but a more effective sales tool is the broker's open, limited to real estate agents from the surrounding area.

STRESS COSMETIC IMPROVEMENT

Not all sellers have time to make surface enhancements to their home, especially if they're making an urgent move, perhaps due to a job transfer. But those with sufficient time and cash generally more than recoup their expenses. Any money you spend on landscaping is especially good for enhancement.

PAINT IS A GOOD INVESTMENT

Like nothing else, paint can brighten up any property interior or exterior. If you need to paint the exterior, you might get some ideas by looking at other houses in the neighborhood. You can tell immediately which color blend is in. One place where you can be a little bolder is the front entrance door. Ideally people should see the door from the street, and a color that pops will help them find it. It's also a good idea to create a welcoming pathway leading to the front door.

SMALL DETAILS

Pay attention to small details! It is often the small things that catch prospective tenants' eyes. Put some plants in containers and use them to showcase the entrance, and for goodness sake, invest in a nice doormat.

I remember going to several beautiful homes and people had the nastiest doormats. Doormats are expected to be dirty. After all, they are used to wipe off your shoes. They are expected to be dirty, but by no means should they be a pile of dirty rags!

RENOVATIONS

Renovation projects can be risky. You don't want to be spending more money than you can recoup on the sale. Think of interior paint as your top priority. Consider picking up a paint roller and painting the rooms in a non-controversial all-tan color.

Learn the art of enhancing a property's appeal to would-be buyers. Enhancing the property is a good investment. You will easily recover all costs selling or renting.

ATTRACTIVE FEATURES

If you want buyers or tenants to pay high prices for your house or apartment, you should include attractive features that will appeal to buyers or tenants on several emotional waves. Remember, small things can be very powerful and pleasing to one's taste. Imagine walking up to an apartment or house, and as you look around, you see dazzling features like an attractive walkway laced with flowers leading up to the property's front entrance. At the entrance, you see a lovely entrance door with an attractive doormat! You enter the home and marvel at the highly polished floors!

Now you can't wait to see the rest! Get my point?

YOUR OWN FLAIR

Don't be afraid to incorporate your own flair and landscaping. Be creative. You might opt to do some of the work yourself. Take these opportunities to be creative and have the landscaping reflect your personality. However, be sure to keep beauty and maintenance in mind.

From a practical standpoint, consider suggestions and strive to create a flexible landscape, one that you can change or upgrade as the landscape takes shape. Choose colorful, perennial flowers that will bloom in the spring and summer, and will be easy to work with in terms of climate, shade, sunlight, maintenance, etc.

Let your flower beds "shine!" Whether you make rows of elaborate designs or decide on simplicity, it should be effective in creating an enticing view. Trees or shrubs are wonderful for shade and privacy, but don't select choices that will include fouling thorns or fruit that will attract more bugs than necessary.

If you decide to hire a professional landscaper, be sure to choose one who will be able to incorporate your ideas into a workable and customized design for maximum use and pleasure.

KITCHEN REMODELING

Don't embark on a large-scale kitchen redo requiring the reconfiguration of appliances and cabinetry. Think of minor remodeling. For example, a new kitchen sink can pay big dividends. For around $2,000 plus the help of a contractor or two (or your handyman), you should be able to add a little luster to update your kitchen, providing potential buyers or renters with a feel for how good the crucial part of the home looks!

BATHROOM

Make minor improvements to a problematic bathroom. Chipped or worn floors or wall tiling in a bathroom is a turnoff to many prospective buyers and renters. It is cost-effective for a home seller or renter to replace the old tile, install a new bathroom toilet or sink, or even lighting, if the old ones look dead. If the bathtub has an out-of-date color such as pastel pink, then consider redoing it with a paint job in white acrylic and a liner that is custom molded to fit.

You have to know when to hold or when to sell.

Trusting individual nature must be considered when making a decision to hold or sell a property. You must figure out what you want to achieve thorough the acquisition of a property. The decision as to what you want to achieve should be fixed in your mind and written down on paper before you make any offer to buy any kind of real estate. Some individuals are looking for cash flow, tax shelter, long-term equity buildup, or whatever. Be clear and positive with your decision. Focus!

Most experts say an experienced real estate investor should consider focusing on achieving cash flow from rental income. However, after you've reached a firm financial footing, you may extend your focus on additional achievements.

In any case, if you want to achieve success in your real estate pursuits, you need to clearly understand that you have to purchase real estate that will contribute to your plans for success. Remember, all properties are unique opportunities, and you can find good deals in all properties. Focus on the best deal that will make the greatest contribution to your success!

ROOM TO WRIGGLE

If you are buying property and are considering selling it in two or three years, consider an interest-only mortgage that guarantees low monthly payments for the first five years. This will give you room to wriggle and the ability to continually swap interest-only mortgages, not only keeping mortgage payments low for a long period, but delaying the day of reckoning when the principle becomes due. One in four new mortgages in the United States is an interest-only loan. This is a very good opportunity for a beginner investor!

FLIPPING

For investors who desire to buy properties, improve them, sell them, then pocket the proceeds and move on to the next deal, buying and flipping is a flipper's bird's nest on the ground. Real estate is bought and sold every day making it a ladder for the real estate investor to move step by step, buy properties and improve them, flip them (sell them) and move on. Investors who flip houses accomplish the same task as real estate agents; however, the flipper's upside profit potential is much higher than an agent's commission. The flipper does not need a license to practice; in fact, you'll be better off without a license. Without being licensed, you'll have more room to wriggle. During your search for a good rental property, keep an eye out for properties that will not make good rental properties but may be ideal to fix up and flip.

Remember it is not easy as it looks on TV to find houses suitable for flipping, and there is a tremendous amount of competition out there, which means that the good buys are gone in a very short time.

You must invest in time that is needed to learn the so-called flipping business. Learn all you can about the industry and don't consider making it a career until you've made double the amount of money in a year that you make in your current job.

Learn about market conditions that influence real estate sales and how long houses are staying on the market before they sell. Learn about houses with the right things wrong, and fix them — things such as entry doors, light fixtures, installing low-voltage outdoor lighting, kitchen countertops, tile floors, and landscaping with mature trees and plants.

Get the house repaired as quick as possible. Every day you own the house costs you money in interest, utilities, taxes and insurance. Make sure no prepayment penalties are required for early payment of the mortgage. Banks make money when buyers hold loans. They lose money when buyers prepay their mortgages.

You'll need to have adequate savings in place to pay the bills while money is flowing out the door for repairs. Consider asking the closing agent for a 25 or 30 day closing date. If it's okay, you'll have room to wriggle. You can get supplies for repairs in place, get your handyman ready to start work, get a 'For Sale' ad in the newspaper (if you don't already have a buyer waiting to grab a good deal).

Another reason to have access to cash is that you'll probably need to hold onto the property for up to three months because of Federal Housing Administration (FHA) anti-flipping regulations. Houses sold less than ninety days after they were purchased aren't eligible for FHA mortgage insurance. Those sold between 91 and 180 days are okay but require an additional, independent appraisal to ensure the sales price is justified. Usually a prepayment penalty is 80% of the balance of the first mortgage, times the interest rate, divided by two. So, if you borrow $100,000 and get a mortgage for 5.75 percent, your prepayment penalty would be $2,300 ($80,000 x 5.75% divided by 2).

I strongly suggest building up your cash reserves. After buying six or seven houses, you won't need a lender anymore, you'll be buying houses for cash. However, getting money is the easy part (see Chapter Seven), the hardest part is finding the houses to buy. Houses suitable for flipping are seldom for sale through Realtors, and they're hardly available through auctions. You have to be vigilant out there on the street. It's not an insider's couch-potato ideology; you need to utilize well-organized time to build a rewarding net worth. I remember when in Detroit, Michigan, I got a bank to delay closing for twenty-five days. I told the lender my wife was in France and would be home shortly. The house was vacant. I made a deal with the seller. I agreed to watch the house if he would agree to let me do some work on the house such as cleaning up and landscaping. He agreed. This strategy gave me time to wriggle. At the time of closing, I had the house almost ready to show. I sold the house approximately twelve days after closing.

VALUE

Make sure you have a clear understanding of the value of the property (see Chapter Two). Purchase it at a good, low price, leaving room for a reasonable profit. Much is at stake. You must find sellers willing to sell their homes 10% to 20% below market value of similar homes in the area. An overpriced property is soon shunned by buyers, which typically leads to a poor outcome for the seller. Don't get stuck trying to sell an overpriced home.

However, if the neighborhood is excellent and the property has outstanding features and curb appeal, you can expect to sell the property 5% or 10% above appraised value.

I accomplished this on two occasions in Detroit, one on a lovely home. I made my exit by allowing my broker to place the home on the market just a notch below the market value. This tactic created a "feeding frenzy" among buyers. They pushed up the price by bidding against each other! This tactic paid off only because the home was a super beautiful home in an upscale community!

Remember, it's up to you to learn the game not taught in real estate schools, especially when it comes to dealing in the real estate buying and selling game. As I stated above, you'll be better off operating without a license. Why? You don't have to worry about complying with many laws, rules and regulations. For example, you may say to a seller who has been trying to sell his property for three or four months, "Well, the reason why your house hasn't sold is because the interest rate is going up." When, in fact, the reason is because the house is in poor condition. Or, the neighborhood is changing and you need to sell. Or, a house just like yours four blocks away sold for $195,000.

To operate with a license, you have to work from an office and adhere to strict rules of conduct, and if anyone registers a complaint that is upheld, you are at risk of losing or having your license suspended.

BEFORE SELLING

You may consider a market analysis report provided by your real estate agent or from the various web sites that claim to provide current values for homes in most areas of the country. One such site, www.Zillow.com, not only provides estimated values but aerial photos of neighborhoods where the property is located, and charts that show value fluctuations over the past week and year. It should be noted that zillow data is quite complete in most areas. Indiana, Texas and Louisiana are left out due to their nondisclosure laws.

PROFESSIONAL APPRAISER

Sometimes properties remain on the market for a long time before a sale is consummated. Therefore, it is wise to consider obtaining a comprehensive report from a professional appraiser before placing your property on the market. It's costly, but offers significant advantages, such as providing a prospective buyer with a credible report on the current market value of the home, thus expediting a decision to purchase the property.

Many beginner real estate investors who wish to sell property are unaware of the rewards from the cost of a professional appraisal. They fail to realize that the appraisal report can be very helpful in moving a sale forward in the market place. A report not only includes details about the property in question, but also adjacent property and a good evaluation of the real estate market in the area. A report also includes detail of major problems with the property that may affect its value and an estimate of the expected time it will take to sell the property. It will give you good insight of important things about how it fits into the market.

PURCHASING A HOME

When you are considering purchasing a home and you find out that a full appraisal has been completed, be sure to ask for and receive that report. On the other hand, if an appraisal was not completed before the sale, remember, there was certainly one ordered during the mortgage processing. Request a copy of the report from your mortgage broker. It's your right under federal law to obtain a copy of the appraisal report.

CHAPTER TEN
GOOD FAITH SETTLEMENT COST

Federal law requires a settlement agent to provide a copy of the home purchaser's settlement sheet and a form known as HUD-1 at least one business day before closing, only if requested to do so by the purchaser.

While some closing agents do deliver the HUD-1 in advance, others fail to provide it even when asked.

LOW BALLING SETTLEMENT FEES

This practice can be especially harmful to you. Diligently shop the mortgage marketplace for the best deals, the lowest interest rates, combined with the lowest closing cost. Some loan officers intentionally give out lowball estimates of fees to get business in the door, and that is a clear deception and a fraudulent trade practice!

Discuss this practice with the mortgage broker you are dealing with (you should have one in your bag, as I pointed out in Chapter Three). I'm sure he or she will definitely give you the best deals possible.

Why? You'll be dealing with this broker consistently, and he wants to keep your business!

COMPLAINTS

The Department of Housing and Urban Development (HUD) gets complaints from many home buyers and refinancers alleging that the disbursements and the final charges on the settlement sheet differ.

UPCHARGES / MARKUPS

HUD's rules prohibit lenders and settlement agents from charging more for appraisals, credit reports, and other third-party services they order unless they provide additional services justifying the higher cost.

For instance, a lender cannot pay $250 for an appraisal and then charge the buyer $450 at closing without performing additional work.

Through my research, I found that several Federal Appellate Courts have ruled against HUD's position.

However, HUD continues to pursue the issue nationwide.

UNLIMITED MARKUPS ALLOWED

Here's a state by state division at the moment: Maryland, Virginia, North and South Carolina, West Virginia, Illinois, Iowa, Wisconsin, Indiana, Minnesota, Missouri, Arkansas, Nebraska, North and South Dakota have no federal protection against markups.

No matter how little your mortgage company paid for documents, tax services, appraisals and messenger services, you need to accept that they are free to charge whatever they think they can squeeze out of you.

NO MARKUPS ALLOWED

Residents of Florida, Georgia, Alabama, New York, Connecticut, Vermont, Pennsylvania, New Jersey, and Delaware live in the current no-markup zone. They can sue lenders and other service providers for markups and expect to prevail in the courts based on appellate court decisions covering their jurisdictions.

AVOID BEING RIPPED OFF

Be sure you ask for the final guaranteed fees up front, even if you're dealing with your regular loan officer. After all, loan officers are in the business and should know what fees to expect.

Next, always request to see the HUD-I settlement sheet in advance. If necessary, remind the loan officers about the federal requirements and insist on timely performance.

Finally, question the fees that you do not understand or did not expect.

If you have any evidence or even a suspicion of hanky panky, let HUD's settlement sleuths do the research for you and act as the detective. Let the HUD know about it by writing to:

RESPA Unit
HUD, 451 Seventh Street SW
Washington, DC 20410
Or visit www.hud.gov.

PREDATORY LENDING

While not all of the many statutes covering mortgage lending define what predatory lending is, a recent HUD study stated it consists of:

1. Engaging in deception or fraud;
2. Manipulating the borrower through aggressive sales tactics;
3. Taking advantage of a borrower's lack of understanding about loan terms; and
4. Loan terms that, alone or in combination, are abusive.

Predatory lending usually occurs when borrowers use the collateral in their homes for debt consolidation or consumer credit.

CLOSING THE TRANSACTION

Real estate closings are nothing more than a meeting for the buyer to deliver the cash and the seller to execute and deliver the deed.

Once the real estate contract has been signed, the closing agent starts his or her engine for the work that needs to be done. All parties to a transaction expect their closing agent, Realtor, title company or attorney to monitor and coordinate all the details of the closing.

CLOSING AGENT

The closing agent must receive the following items when the title insurance order is placed.

1. A properly signed and dated contract of sale.
2. A previous title insurance policy on the property.
3. Enough information about the seller, buyer, property, and lender to process and close the transaction.
4. The seller's and buyer's marital status.
5. A complete legal description of the property.
6. Street address including zip code.
7. Terms of any purchase-money mortgage the title company must prepare.
8. Closing date and information about whether all parties will attend.
9. Commission, if any.

ORDER A TITLE SEARCH

The closing agents, after ensuring that all necessary information is in the file, will then order a title search.

EVIDENCE OF TITLE

There are two principal methods of giving a buyer evidence of the title: one is abstract or title insurance; the abstract would then be used by an attorney to give an opinion of title.

Abstracting is becoming obsolete. With the development of microfilm, photocopying, computers and the internet, copies of the actual documents can be inspected.

OPINION OF TITLE

An opinion of the title is an attorney's professional opinion of the condition of the title, based on his or her examination of the title. If, at a later date, the title is found to be defective, the buyer may find it difficult to recover from the damage done by finding an undisclosed name on the ownership or an undisclosed lien. That's why it is so important to get a real estate attorney to work on your behalf.

TITLE INSURANCE

Title insurance is the dominant method used by buyers and lenders to protect their interests. Title insurance will pay for losses sustained, and the owner does not have to prove negligence.

The two basic types of title insurance are: owner's title insurance and lender's title insurance. As you'll find in most insurance policies, there are exclusions and exceptions.

EXCLUSIONS IN THE TITLE INSURANCE POLICY

Exclusions arise mainly from actions that the government has the power to take, such as eminent domain (see Glossary). Exactly which exclusions are present in the title insurance depends on the type of insurance policy. A standard coverage policy normally insures the title as it is known from the public records. It also insures against hidden defects such as forged documents, conveyance by incompetent grantors, incorrect marital statements, and improperly delivered deeds.

An extended coverage policy such as an American Land Title Policy (ALTA) gives more coverage. For instance, it will protect against the facts that may be discovered by a property inspector, and rights of parties in possession, examination of a survey, and certain unrecorded liens.

MOST LENDERS REQUIRE LENDERS ATLA POLICY

Like most insurance policies, there are exclusions and exceptions from the insurance. These exclusions arise mainly from government restrictions on ownership (police power, eminent domain, and ad valorem taxation) and private restrictions (deed restrictions, leases, lien, and easements). These exclusions arise mainly from actions that the government has the power to take, such as eminent domain (see Glossary).

STANDARD EXCLUSIONS

A title insurance policy does not cover the following:
1. Police power of the government, such as the zoning and building restrictions, etc.
2. Rights of eminent domain;
3. Liens or encumbrances created by the insured person, or those known to the insured person at the time of purchase, but not known by the title insurance company.

EXCEPTIONS

Some policy exceptions would include:
1. Rights of a party in possession of the properties that are not shown in the public records. This would include a rental tenant;
2. Encroachments that could have been found if the survey had been made;
3. Items not shown in the public records, such as old roadways on the property;
4. Construction liens and rights not shown in the public records;
5. Ad valorem taxes or special assessments not shown as existing liens.
6. Restrictive covenants.

PAYOFF LETTER

The closing agent must send for the mortgage payoff letter and check with public records for information on taxes and special assessments.

LOAN PACKAGE

The lender sends all documents and closing instructions in a loan package. The loan documents are checked for names, legal description, and loan amount. The closing agent must follow the lender's instructions exactly or contracts can be liable for hundreds of dollars per day until corrections are made.

HUD-1 SETTLEMENT STATEMENT

Before the closing, the agent must distribute the HUD-1 closing statement. The title closing agent must certify that the statement is a true and accurate statement of the transaction, and that the funds will be disbursed according to the statement.

The title company may require affidavits from the buyer, seller and real state licensee that there are no hidden mortgages, borrowed closing funds, or any illegal agreements.

THE CLOSING

The closing agent must notify all parties of the date and time of closing. The amount due from the buyer should be in the form of a certified check to speed up disbursement. The closing agent will, if need be, check with the licensee for any task that still needs to be done such as a wood-destroying organism inspection.

PROOFREADING THE CLOSING PACKAGE

The final part of the closing preparation is a complete review of the closing package. At the closing, each party must agree on the accuracy of the names, dates, legal description, loan information, loan closing costs, fees for recording the documents, stamps, taxes, intangible taxes, discount points, origination fees, broker's commission (if any), survey, and inspections.

GETTING CLOSING DOCUMENTS TO THE PARTIES BEFORE CLOSING!

All parties should receive and proofread the closing documents prior to closing. As a buyer, you'll have an opportunity to check all the paperwork before the closing.

AT THE CLOSING TABLE

The closing normally includes the buyer, the seller, and their respective agents, if any. Sometimes closings are attended by the attorneys of the parties, and sometimes by a lender's representative. The closing agent conducts the closing.

SEPARATE CLOSINGS

Some closing agents and real estate agents prefer that the buyer and seller close separately rather than at the same closing table. This reduces or eliminates disputes and allows the closing agent to focus on each of the parties as they close. Sometimes, when the buyer or seller lives out of town, separate closings occur, and the closing package with the signatures of one party is mailed to the other party living out of town.

THE WARRANTY DEED

The warranty deed is the document that transfers ownership of the real property. The warranty deed is the most common deed by which the seller guarantees to the buyer that he has good title without material defects or encumbrances, and will stand by the guarantee forever.

THE SALES CONTRACT

The sales contract is a very, very important document. It is the foundation that supports all other documents and serves as proof. It is a bilateral contract, or a two-way agreement. It is both the foundation and the chemical reaction of buying and selling real estate.

The seller agrees to sell and the purchaser agrees to buy. The sales contract embodies the terms for the transfer of real state, and requires the signature of both buyer and seller.

RESPONSIBILITY FOR PREPARATION
"'Not me,' said the inexperienced investor"

A sales contract must be prepared with skill, care and diligence. If you are not certain about the contract or wording for any special clause, the safest course of action is to get help from your faithful real estate agent or consult an experienced real estate attorney.

This contract must be prepared correctly and express the complete intent of the parties. Remember, if any errors, omissions or ambiguities exist regarding material terms, the contract will not go outside the contents of the contract to decide intent.

The person who prepared the contract will not be allowed to explain later as to the intent not shown in the contents of the contract.

EARNEST MONEY DEPOSIT

The buyer usually makes a deposit called earnest money to bind the contract and to show good faith. The law requires no specific amount of earnest money. Therefore, when you are buying, put down as little as possible ($200 to $500). When you are selling, you should get as much as possible ($1,000 to $5,000). The amount of earnest money reflects the motivation of the parties and the length of time until closing.

ESCROW FUNDS

As the buyer, it is wise to have earnest money held in escrow by an escrow agent or a title company of your choice. Never let the seller hold the escrow. However, when you are the seller, do just the opposite—keep the earnest money in your account or with a title company of your choice.

If the contract calls for an additional deposit, the amounts and the number of days within which it is to be made should be inserted. As a buyer, if you fail to make the additional deposit, it is a default and the seller may recover not only the initial deposit but also any unpaid deposit.

DISCLOSURE RIDERS

Contract "riders" are contract additions made necessary as circumstances dictate. Various laws and regulations require that some riders be attached to the contract. Remember, it depends on the circumstances.

CONDOMINIUM RIDER

Be sure the printed clauses of the contract do not contain any specific provisions related to the sale and purchase of the condominium units.

VA/FHA RIDER

This rider becomes necessary because transactions involving VA or FHA financing include many unique elements.

HOMEOWNER ASSOCIATION DISCLOSURE

With this disclosure, riders should be given to the buyers if there is a homeowners association that can place a lien on the property for nonpayment of homeowner dues, or has restrictive covenants regulating the use and occupancy of the property.

"AS IS" RIDER

This means that the buyer agrees to take the property without warranties and knows about its condition. However, the rider does not relieve the seller of the duty to disclose material defects in the property he knows will affect the value of the property.

LEAD BASE PAINT RIDER

This disclosure is required for all homes built before 1978.

INSULATION RIDER

The Federal Trade Commission requires this rider when the sale involves newly improved residential real estate property. It must show that the insulation has been installed or will be installed in walls, ceilings and other areas.

THE WINDING ROAD TO CLOSING

CHAPTER ELEVEN
PROPERTY MANAGEMENT

Poor property management is like feeding a bulldog that is chasing you. I can, with my experience, diagnose an ailing real estate investment property, large or small, and its failing problems without spending one penny on research. Complete answers can be found right smack dab in the hands of property management!

Effective property management means you can't just pull money out of your property; you must also put money back into it. Property management is one of the most important aspects of real estate investments. Property management is where most of the profits are made.

IT'S NOT WHAT YOU DO, IT'S THE WAY YOU DO IT!

Buying, renting or flipping real estate does not assure financial success. It's not what you do, it's the way that you do it. That's what gets results. That should be embodied in the overall investment plans and procedures that lead to the closing table and to the bank!

Good management begets good cash flows, waves after wave after wave, pushing you straight to financial independence. The idea that property management is not important is a brain-dead idea.

BE PREPARED FOR PROPERTY MANAGEMENT

Many landlords are not prepared to manage a property. They are not equipped with the basic knowledge to handle rental properties, and don't know whom to call for help. That's where this book comes in. It will teach you to analyze your abilities, and you can improve yourself if need be.

PROPERTY MANAGEMENT COMPANY

If you decide to hire a management company to handle your rental units, be sure to look for a company with a long track record in the real estate sector. Choose a company close to your area with good management abilities.

Regardless of whether you manage a property or have outside management do it, you will want to know for sure that the job will be done well with regard to the handling of advertising, marketing, collection and accounting, etc.

GOOD ENVIRONMENT

Remember, good tenants want to live in an environment that gives them a feeling of getting their money's worth, even if they pay a little more in rent. With this kind of interaction, you will be helping the tenant as well as yourself. (And that's the way you do it!)

By making the tenant feel good, content and satisfied, when they move they most likely will recommend a friend of theirs to you, and the beat goes on ... wave after wave after wave. Sometimes, tenants living in nearby buildings will want to move into your building.

What you sow is what you get back on those waves. Therefore, good management and excellent upkeep will help keep the property rented, attract good tenants, get the highest rent, help ensure rents are paid on time, improve tenant relations, and keep operating costs down. Low operating costs means higher cash flow.

RENT COLLECTION

If you have outside management services, never allow your management company to accept cash for rent. Only in an emergency should you, and only you, accept cash from a tenant. Always insist on tenants paying rent with checks or money orders. This eliminates the opportunity for theft or even embezzlement of your income.

INCREASE IN VALUE

Good management and upkeep will definitely increase the value of your property in just a few months after acquisition, and consequently, your cash flow as well. Many real estate investors hate to be involved in managing property. They simply hate to be connected with the management process, but it is highly profitable and greatly rewarding when you take the helm and control your own destiny.

Take the case of Donald Trump, one of the world's greatest real estate investors. He turned property management into his personal art form and made it a core element of his overall real estate investing strategy. His approach to property management involves treating it as a customer-service business, and he sees tenants as valued customers. As a result, he is able to generate huge profits with his management strategies.

MANAGE THE RIGHT WAY

Managing real estate the right way is no accident. You must fill yourself with knowledge, discipline and will power! Get a new attitude, and don't be contaminated by the concession of old, funky attitudes.

MAINTENANCE

If you are a beginner, starting off with little money (as I did), you will be smart to do most of your own repairs and management. You'll save thousands of dollars, and could be the landlord, gardener and handyman while holding a full-time job!

When I started, I knew nothing about plumbing, electrical repairs, or anything else. I purchased a tool box in 1965 (I still have that toolbox!) to keep my tools together. If you are a beginning investor with little capital, I suggest you go to Home Depot or some similar store and purchase a tool box, some basic tools, and basic books on plumbing, electrical repairs and carpentry. All you need are the basics. You are not trying to become an expert or professional.

It doesn't matter if you just got out of college with a degree in whatever line of study. If you want to become financially wealthy, you must start thinking about investing in something to provide a jumpstart for extra cash flow ... hopefully a large amount.

I'm not talking about becoming a workaholic, but don't be afraid to get your hands dirty. Get with it and have that extra cash flow coming in wave after wave after wave.

GETTING ESTABLISHED

When you get established, you'll be in a position to hire service companies to do most of the work for you. That's what I did. To use a good, reliable company, I suggest a small company close to your area. Get to know them and stick with them. If you are out of town or out of the country, there'll be no problem; they'll do the necessary work for you and put it on your account (or should I say, put it on the tenants' account, because they are the ones who will pay the account).

At this point in time, if you own several properties, you can put 100% of your paycheck in the bank and your income from your properties will cover all of your costs and living expenses (tax free).

DO LESS MAINTENANCE WORK

Now, when you own several properties, you can throw your tool chest and books away. You'll be moving up the ladder to a higher step, and you will be in a position to do less maintenance work; your handyman will do most of, if not all, the small jobs.

Your contractor will do the extensive work. But you'll still be on the scene, mostly with a note pad and pen instead of a hammer and monkey wrench!

PRE-RENTAL CHECK

Whenever you purchase a property for rental purposes or to flip, check it out carefully before you flip it or rent it to tenants. Check all water faucets to make sure they are not dripping. Flush all toilets and make sure they're operating effectively. Know where the main valve and water meter are located so that you, your tenant or a service person can cut off incoming water to the property if need be. Check electrical outlet receptacles and switches. Check all appliances.

HANDYMAN

If you feel a little doubtful, locate a handyman with experience to assist you in all your work, especially during pre-rental inspections. For a small fee, the handyman will go through the property with you and check things out. You'll learn a lot this way (if you haven't learned a lot already).

In other words, this pre-rental inspection will prevent problems before they show their ugly faces. Remember, small problems, if neglected, could become major repair jobs, consequently reducing your cash flow.

GET RECEIPTS

Get receipts for everything you buy or pay for. Everything you pay for, large or small, is tax deductible. Keep your receipts in order. Each property should have its own file; this way you can see exactly what's being spent on any particular property.

GOOD TENANTS TAKE CARE OF PROPERTY

Some tenants take better care of rental property (especially houses) than some homeowners. Anything you can do to encourage good house-keeping is well worth your efforts. You could supply some materials such as paint, flowers to plant, and tools to work with, especially if you're renting a house instead of an apartment.

In any case, make a good impression by going out of your way to set up favorable cohesiveness. Give tenants a list of schools, churches, parks, post offices, banks, libraries, supermarkets and other useful services that are close by if they are new to the area.

MAKE TENANTS FEEL AT HOME

Tenants feel at home when they take part in some of the upkeep of the property. It gives them the feeling that your house is their house, a place to live for a long time! Have your handyman install a special lighting fixture or mirror for ladies to do their make-up. There are many small items that will mean a lot to tenants. People like them even if it means paying more rent!

TENANTS PAY FOR SOME UPKEEP

Having tenants agree to pay for some minor repairs will encourage the feeling of having a stake in the property. Let the tenant take part in making out the rental agreement and the lease. The lease may say (and the tenant has agreed) that the tenant will change filters in the furnace or cooling unit at his/her expense, cut the grass, maintain the yard, or repair leaky faucets.

Tenants should also agree to use your handyman for the minor repairs.

INSURANCE

Always carry fire and hazard insurance on all your properties. If you know you are going to flip a property in fifteen or twenty days, you may pass on the insurance, but even if you plan to flip a property that needs a lot of repair work, you should get liability insurance.

RENTER'S INSURANCE

Remind your tenants that they need renter's insurance (include this need in their lease or application). Let the tenants know that the landlord is not responsible for loss or damage to their personal property. Renter's insurance protects tenants' personal possessions if their property gets damaged, destroyed or stolen. Let them know that their live-in honey doesn't get automatic insurance coverage on his or her stuff based on their individual renter's policy.

Give your new tenants a list of three or four companies that offer renter's insurance. Better yet, give them the names of several agents. This way you'll be improving your contacts. (Get what I mean?)

CHAPTER TWELVE
NUTS AND BOLTS OF A HOME INSPECTION

Most states have laws or court decisions requiring written home defect disclosures. When a home seller discloses known defects such as a leaky roof or a noisy barking dog next door, the buyer has no legal grounds for a fraud or misrepresentation law suit after the sale closes.

Selling or buying "as is" is perfectly legal in most states, when the defects are disclosed before the sale. If you are buying property with costly defects, the seller may allow estimated costs to be deducted from the selling price. For instance, the repairs might cost $6,000. You have your handyman who will do the work for $4,000. Or, you may be dealing with a good remodeling company that gives you a great discount on all your jobs.

In any case, you can save big money on repairs by using the same company over and over.

One of the most effective ways to make sure that the property you are buying is in good condition is to include in the purchase contract a contingent clause for a home inspection report prepared for you by a qualified home inspector. When performed properly, the inspection should disclose material defects in a building that buyers, sellers and real estate agents might miss.

You are encouraged to select your own inspector. This way, you can be assured the inspector is a member of the American Society of Home Inspectors.

INSPECTING THE EXTERIOR

Most inspectors will start their inspections at the curb, right in front of the house. The inspector will evaluate the topography of the site. If the ground slopes toward the house or garage, it might result in water seepage. The ground near the perimeter of the house should be graded away from the house so that water does not settle in the foundation area. In hilly areas, the water flow may be more of a problem, and water may actually enter the building during periods of heavy rain.

PAVED AREAS

The principal cause of damage to driveways and sidewalks is tree roots. The solution to uneven sections of the sidewalk and broken driveway pavement is to cut away the tree roots and repair the pavement.

Asphalt driveways deteriorate in harsh weather and may need to be patched and resealed to preserve their life. Concrete walkways sometimes settle because the base below the sidewalk was improperly prepared.

WALLS

An inspection of the exterior walls includes examining doors and windows. The inspector will generally gauge the uniformity of the wall surface, and look for cracking or sagging. Window and door lines should be square. Cracks at the corners of doors or windows may be evidence of more serious settling problems.

SIDING

The bottom of the siding should be well above ground level to reduce the chance of rot or termite infestation.

Wood siding is subject to deterioration if neglected, requiring extensive repairs. Whenever the siding joins masonry or metal, there is a greater likelihood of water penetration and rot. Unfinished wood siding is subject to mildew and water stains.

ALUMINUM SIDING AND VINYL SIDING

Aluminum siding and vinyl siding are both relatively maintenance free. Aluminum siding should be inspected for dents. It is only a cosmetic problem and will not affect the durability.

TRIM

Trim includes the molding around doors and windows, the shutters, the sofits (under roof eaves), and the fascia. The trim is untreated wood and is subject to rot. It should be carefully inspected around the roof, around the molding at the edge of the roof, the molding around garage doors, and sliding doors on patios where the water splashes during rain.

WINDOWS

All bedrooms should have at least one operable window with a seal no higher than 42" to allow for an emergency exit (not to mention the law in most states is that the window should not be less than 18").

DOORS

Some exterior doors have glass areas too close to the door lock, making it easy to break in. The inspector will usually recommend that a deadbolt lock be installed.

Doors should be checked for rot at the top and bottom, and for proper operation. Weather stripping should also be recommended.

ROOF

The inspector must examine both the roof covering, such as shingles, and the decking on pitched roofs. The inspector will check the condition of the covering from the exterior and the decking from the attic. Uneven and sagging seams from the exterior may be evidence of structural problems, and a professional may be needed to evaluate the condition.

Areas around chimneys, vents and skylights sometimes leak because of poorly installed or deteriorating flashing.

GARAGE

If the garage is attached to the house, the doorway leading to the house must be fire resistant and have a tight seal around the walls, ceilings and doors, and walls should be inspected for leaks, stains and/or patches.

The inspector checks to see if the ornamental garage door opener works, and whether it has an automatic reversing feature to protect children or pets, if it should close on them.

INTERIOR

Be sure to check the attic for adequate insulation. Attic ventilation is important, so vent openings should be clear. If the attic is poorly ventilated, the plywood might deteriorate. Plumbing pipes should not terminate in the attic. Air conditioning ducts should be checked to ensure that there are no open joints allowing cooled or heated air to escape.

Roof sheathing should be checked for evidence of leaks.

AIR CONDITIONING AND HEATING

The compressor unit should discharge warm air while operating. It should be clear and level, and the airflow area clear of obstruction. The condensation drain line should be clear of debris to prevent water backing up and leaking on ceiling or walls.

The air vents should be clear of obstruction.

ELECTRICAL SYSTEMS

The wire from the electrical service pole will be attached to the house at 10' above the ground in most states. There will be two or three wires. If only two wires are coming in, the electrical service is probably inadequate. Two wires indicates 110 volts service. Three wires usually provide the needed 110/120 volts service.

Modern homes should have at least 200 AMP electrical services.

PLUMBING

The water supply system will commonly have a shutoff valve so the water can be turned off for the entire house. The location of the shutoff valve should be shown to the buyer. The inspector should check and operate all fixtures.

If water pressure is low, it could indicate that some lines are blocked from corrosion. Sink drains should open and close properly.

The inspector will check water heaters for adequate size and recovery rates for the size of the house.

INTERIOR ROOMS

Rooms that have cracked walls and lined door jams may be an indication of structural problems. Sometimes, the damage may be caused by water leakage. Ceiling discoloration or peeling paint is evidence of water intrusion.

BATHROOM

Bathrooms should have adequate ventilation. Bathrooms with no windows should have an operating vent and a fan. The fan should vent to the outside to avoid excess mildew buildup in the attic. Fixtures should have separate shutoff valves.

CONTINGENT CLAUSE

A contingent clause is a powerful negotiation tool to have included in your purchase contract. Any defects found will give you room to wriggle (negotiate a lower price).

You can also use the inspection clause to kill a deal that turns out to be a bad choice. If the seller refuses to make the necessary repairs or adjustment to the price, you can cancel the contract and receive your deposit back.

On the other hand, if you're planning to flip the property to another, you may consider having a clause in the contract that allows you access to the property at reasonable times so you can show it to prospective buyers. You may have the property sold before you buy it. It has happened, and I'm a witness. However, I won't go into detail. But I will repeat— there are more ways than one to skin a cat, and you don't learn how to skin a cat in a real estate school.

In any case, consider using the contingency clause in a new contract. Remember, you'll have a certain amount of time to inspect the property. After the inspection, you should provide the seller with the inspection report, and give the seller time to respond.

CHAPTER THIRTEEN
A MAP FOR YOUR RETIREMENT FUTURE

Whether you're getting started in your first job, first investment property, or getting ready to exit the work force, this chapter will help you take charge of your destiny by establishing a solid base to put enough money away to enjoy whatever you like in retirement.

A GUIDE

Here's a guide to what needs to be done at every age. Everyone needs a compass to point them in the right direction and to do things that need their attention. Many people finish their schooling at age 21 or 24. Others remain students well into their thirties (or forties like I did); whatever your situation is, you need the following guide.

YEARS GETTING YOURSELF ESTABLISHED

If you are 25 to 35 years of age, this is the stage of life when most people's schooling is finished. Hopefully, your career is blossoming but you haven't reached your peak yet. You may be just starting a career or changing jobs. This is the time to put your brakes on and establish sound financial habits to last a lifetime (yes, that's right, a lifetime).

Investing will be an important task in the years ahead, and this is the time to learn and try out all you can, even if you can't afford to invest much.

TASK

- Establish credit. Pay off balances every month except for car loans and home mortgage.
- Establish a habit of automatic savings for short-term retirement.
- Set up an emergency savings fund.

- Establish relationships with financial advisors, a financial planner, accountants and attorney.
- Make a will, especially if you have children or a spouse.
- If you can, buy a home. Home ownership is a tax advantage and investment (it will grow in value). Obviously, some people prefer to rent, but a home is the backbone of personal wealth in many American households.
- Make sure you have adequate life, disability, automobile, health and homeowners insurance.
- Talk to your employer and make sure you're taking full advantage of the benefits available to you.
- If you have children, begin saving for their education.

HOW TO GET THEM DONE
- Make sure your credit payments are on time.
- Consult a lawyer to write your will.
- Establish an IRA account or Keogh plan for retirement investment.
- Read at least one investment book every year.

AGE 35 - 45
You will be, without a doubt, coping with a variety of high expenses, especially if you have a growing family. Your income will grow as you advance in your career. Your investment experience and expertise should grow too.

As your earnings grow, so do your expenses. Your children's education needs and your need for retirement savings may combine to outstrip your income.

TASK
- As your income increases, look for prudent ways to shelter part of it from taxes.
- Make sure your insurance is up to date and adequate.
- Consult an attorney.
- Make sure your will is up to date.
- If you have children, continue their educational savings.
- Continue to keep your credit under control and avoid paying finance charges.

HOW TO GET THEM DONE

- Get financial help to review tax savings proposals.
- Explore the opportunity of investing in rental properties.
- Take full advantage of your IRA, 401k, and other tax advantage retirement plans.
- If you're self employed, establish a Keogh plan or separate IRA.
- If you are in debt, consider a home equity loan in which you deduct interest payments.
- Take periodic inventories of your belongings for insurance purposes.
- Revise your will if necessary.
- Consult a financial adviser to determine whether you need an estate plan, a strategy for leaving assets to your heirs with the least bite from federal estate taxes.
- Strongly consider making investments that require your active participation, such as owning rental property.

AGE 45 - 55

Get serious about saving for your retirement. This is the stage in life (according to experts) where people typically become net savers instead of net borrowers. As children make their exits from the nest, your cost for housing, food, clothing and other items may decline (though your savings could be more than offset by education bills).

This is the time to start thinking about retirement, and to capitalize on your investment experience and expertise, especially in rental property. Of course, it's also time to start seriously thinking about your own future plans.

TASK

- Maximize your savings for retirement.
- Establish or revise your estate plan.
- Make sure your growing assets are protected by liability insurance, especially your rental properties.
- Take full advantage of employee benefits such as stock purchase or profit sharing plans.
- Make any necessary provisions for the care of your children, parents and other dependents in the event of your death.

HOW TO GET THEM DONE

- Increase your regular payments to retirement savings with extra cash you save once debts are paid off with any pay increases you get.
- Meet with your attorney to review your will and make sure it is up to date. Do the same with your estate plan.
- With help from a financial planner and calculator, determine what resources would be available to your dependents if you died.

OPTIONAL RECOMMENDATIONS

- Continue learning about investments, and find ways to put what you learn into practice, especially real estate investments.
- If you own a business, consider what you want to happen when you can no longer run it.
- Start thinking of what you'd like to do in retirement, and do whatever you can to plan for it.

AGE 55 - 65

Think defensively and take big steps to protect what you've amassed. Now that you have more time and financial resources to devote to yourself, your key job is to protect your assets and stay the course toward retirement.

TASK

- Review your will and estate planning.
- When you get within four years of retirement, start shifting some of your investments to more conservative options such as bonds and real estate investments.
- Do more serious planning for retirement.
- Pay off all your debts, with the possible exception of a home mortgage or rental property.

HOW TO GET THEM DONE

- Have your attorney review your will and recommend any steps that will reduce estate taxes.
- Pay off or reduce the loans on your primary residence, and leave the rental property as is.

- Estimate your financial needs and resources at retirement.
- Consider moving to a smaller home or a new location to reduce living costs.
- Consider what activities you'll want to pursue in retirement, and look for ways to prepare for them.
- Make sure your estate planning is done by an accountant or lawyer, not a sales agent.

AGE 65 OR OLDER

Exit signs are hanging on all doors, even the toilet. You know that the time is nearing for you to make your last exit. If you've followed the above recommendations, you should be in a very good position to gracefully walk through the nearest exit door, waving goodbye with both hands. Don't be caught up in the so-called life expectancy increasing syndrome and Social Security facing an uncertain future.

You'll need all the resources you can muster to live the way you want. If you do your homework, as pointed out in this book and in this chapter, you will be way ahead. With some real estate investments in your portfolio, anybody can retire at age 50 or 52 (as I did).

TASK

- Switch a substantial part of your investments to low-risk types such as real estate rental properties, bonds, and mutual funds designed to produce income instead of growth.
- Complete estate planning.
- Protect your assets from financial schemes aimed at seniors.
- Maintain your health and long-term care insurance.

HOW TO GET THEM DONE

- Consult a financial adviser to make sure your investments are appropriate for your needs.
- Keep growth investments as a hedge against inflation.
- Revise your will so it is appropriate for your current circumstances.
- Be wary of offers, especially telephone solicitations that seem too good to be true. Consult someone you trust before you commit to anything.

APPENDICES

ACCEPTANCE OF PARTIAL PAYMENT
AND NON-WAIVER AGREEMENT

Date: _____
Owner: _____
Tenant: _____
Address: _____

I/we the undersigned, acknowledge that my/our rent was due and payable on the ____ day of _____, 19__. In accordance with my/our Rental Agreement, I/We understand this constituted a breach, and could cause termination of our occupancy and legal action by management. I/We understand that the total rent due and owing is $_____, which includes any and all unpaid rent and any properly assessed late charges in the amount of $_____. I/We wish to pay this amount in the following manner:

_____
_____
_____
_____
_____
_____

I/We understand and agree that management does not waive its right under the law or under my/our Rental Agreement. I/We reaffirm my/our agreement to pay rent not later than the _____ day of each month, and understand and agree that failure to pay any of the amounts stated above by the dates so specified shall cause all of said amounts to become immediately due and payable in full and also entitle management to immediately commence legal proceedings, tough forcible detainer action, without further demand of notice.

_____
Resident

_____
Resident

Received this _____ day of _____, 19___.

By: _____, Manager

PROPERTY INTERIOR CHECKLIST

Kitchen	OK	NOT	Additional Comments
Floors clean	[ ]	[ ]	
Disposal	[ ]	[ ]	
Sink stopper	[ ]	[ ]	
Strainer	[ ]	[ ]	
Sink chips	[ ]	[ ]	
Countertops	[ ]	[ ]	
Range hood lean	[ ]	[ ]	
Cabinets	[ ]	[ ]	
Exhaust fan works	[ ]	[ ]	
Dishwasher	[ ]	[ ]	
---Serial #	[ ]	[ ]	
Refrigerator	[ ]	[ ]	
---Serial #	[ ]	[ ]	
---Clean	[ ]	[ ]	
---Light OK	[ ]	[ ]	
---Trays OK	[ ]	[ ]	
---Shelves OK	[ ]	[ ]	
Range	[ ]	[ ]	
---Serial #	[ ]	[ ]	
---Interior clean	[ ]	[ ]	
---Knobs OK	[ ]	[ ]	
---Pans/racks OK	[ ]	[ ]	
Light switches	[ ]	[ ]	
Bulbs	[ ]	[ ]	
Windows	[ ]	[ ]	
Screens	[ ]	[ ]	
Door	[ ]	[ ]	
Walls	[ ]	[ ]	
Overall clean	[ ]	[ ]	
Other:			
	[ ]	[ ]	
	[ ]	[ ]	
Dining/Living			
Floors	[ ]	[ ]	
Carpets	[ ]	[ ]	
Lights	[ ]	[ ]	
Windows	[ ]	[ ]	
Screens	[ ]	[ ]	
Walls	[ ]	[ ]	
Wood paneling	[ ]	[ ]	
Drapes	[ ]	[ ]	
Drapery rods	[ ]	[ ]	
Other:			
	[ ]	[ ]	
	[ ]	[ ]	

PROPERTY INTERIOR CHECKLIST (continued)

Bathroom(s)	OK	NOT	Additional Comments
First	[ ]	[ ]	_____
Toilet	[ ]	[ ]	_____
Faucets	[ ]	[ ]	_____
Sink chips	[ ]	[ ]	_____
Toilet Paper Roll	[ ]	[ ]	_____
Stoppers work	[ ]	[ ]	_____
Mirrors	[ ]	[ ]	_____
Bars	[ ]	[ ]	_____
Curtain Rods	[ ]	[ ]	_____
Fixtures	[ ]	[ ]	_____
Tile	[ ]	[ ]	_____
Tub caulking	[ ]	[ ]	_____
Tub chips	[ ]	[ ]	_____
Bulbs	[ ]	[ ]	_____
Switches	[ ]	[ ]	_____
Vent fan works	[ ]	[ ]	_____
Floors	[ ]	[ ]	_____
Windows	[ ]	[ ]	_____
Other:			
_____	[ ]	[ ]	_____
_____	[ ]	[ ]	_____

Bedrooms
First

	OK	NOT	
Walls	[ ]	[ ]	_____
Floors	[ ]	[ ]	_____
Carpets	[ ]	[ ]	_____
Lights	[ ]	[ ]	_____
Windows	[ ]	[ ]	_____
Screens	[ ]	[ ]	_____
Closets	[ ]	[ ]	_____
Other:			
_____	[ ]	[ ]	_____
_____	[ ]	[ ]	_____

Second

	OK	NOT	
Walls	[ ]	[ ]	_____
Floors	[ ]	[ ]	_____
Carpets	[ ]	[ ]	_____
Lights	[ ]	[ ]	_____
Windows	[ ]	[ ]	_____
Screens	[ ]	[ ]	_____
Closets	[ ]	[ ]	_____
Other:			
_____	[ ]	[ ]	_____
_____	[ ]	[ ]	_____

PROPERTY INTERIOR CHECKLIST (continued)

Third	OK	NOT	Additional Comments
Walls	[ ]	[ ]	_____
Floors	[ ]	[ ]	_____
Carpets	[ ]	[ ]	_____
Lights	[ ]	[ ]	_____
Windows	[ ]	[ ]	_____
Screens	[ ]	[ ]	_____
Closets	[ ]	[ ]	_____
Other:			
_____	[ ]	[ ]	_____
_____	[ ]	[ ]	_____

Fourth			
Walls	[ ]	[ ]	_____
Floors	[ ]	[ ]	_____
Carpets	[ ]	[ ]	_____
Lights	[ ]	[ ]	_____
Windows	[ ]	[ ]	_____
Screens	[ ]	[ ]	_____
Closets	[ ]	[ ]	_____
Other:			
_____	[ ]	[ ]	_____
_____	[ ]	[ ]	_____

PROPERTY EXTERIOR CHECKLIST

Tenant Name _____

Property Address _____

Move-out Date _____

Comments: _____

_____

_____

_____

_____

_____

	OK	NOT	Additional Comments
Garage	[ ]	[ ]	_____
Carport	[ ]	[ ]	_____
Patio	[ ]	[ ]	_____
Storage Room	[ ]	[ ]	_____
Doors	[ ]	[ ]	_____
---Louvers intact	[ ]	[ ]	_____
---Locks	[ ]	[ ]	_____
---Latches	[ ]	[ ]	_____
---Surfaces	[ ]	[ ]	_____
---Doorstops	[ ]	[ ]	_____
Nameholders	[ ]	[ ]	_____
Doorbell	[ ]	[ ]	_____
Washer	[ ]	[ ]	_____
---Serial #	[ ]	[ ]	_____
---Hookup	[ ]	[ ]	_____
Dryer	[ ]	[ ]	_____
---Serial #	[ ]	[ ]	_____
---Hookup	[ ]	[ ]	_____
Other:			
_____	[ ]	[ ]	_____
_____	[ ]	[ ]	_____

General Remarks: _____

_____

General Remarks: _____

_____

I/We have inspected the above facilities and agree they are in good working condition except as noted.

_____   _____

Tenant   Date

_____   _____

Tenant   Date

HOLD HARMLESS AGREEMENT FOR MOVING TENANT

In consideration of moving, including labor without charge, and the dropping of the eviction costs and fees, _____ (Tenant) do hereby hold Landlord and his agents harmless from any claims for damage incurred in said move.

_____ (Tenant) further releases Landlord and his agents from any and all claims as a result of tenancy.

_____   _____
Tenant   Date

_____   _____
Witnessed by   Date

NOTICE OF TERMINATION

To: _____

        _____

        _____

You are advised that your lease is terminated effective immediately. You shall have 7 days from the delivery of his letter to vacate the premises. This action is taken because:

Dated: _____

                                    _____
                                    Owner or Property Manager

CERTIFICATE OF SERVICE

I hereby certify that a copy of the above notice was delivered to the above-named tenant on the   day of   , 200__, by:

[ ] Personal delivery

[ ] Certified Mail

[ ] Posting on the premises

                                    _____
                                    Owner or Property Manager

THREE-DAY NOTICE

To: _____

          _____

          _____

You are hereby notified that you are indebted to me in the sum of $ dollars for the rent and use of e premises known as
now occupied by you, and that I demand payment of the rent or possession of the premises within 3 days (excluding Saturday, Sunday, and legal holidays) from the date of delivery of this notice, to wit: on or before the   day of   , 200__.

Dated: _____

_____

Signature of Landlord

_____

Type or print Name of Landlord

_____

Address

_____

Telephone number

CERTIFICATE OF SERVICE

I hereby certify that a copy of the above notice was delivered to the above-named tenant on the   day of   , 200__, by:

[ ] Personal delivery

[ ] Certified Mail

[ ] Posting on the premises

_____

Owner or Property Manager

SEVEN-DAY NOTICE

To: _____

         _____

         _____

You are hereby notified that you have violated your rental agreement as follows:

Demand is hereby made that you remedy the noncompliance within 7 days of receipt of this notice or your lease shall be deemed terminated and you shall vacate the premises upon such termination. If this same conduct or conduct of a similar nature is repeated within 12 months, your tenancy is subject to termination without your being given an opportunity to cure the noncompliance.

Dated: _____

_____
Owner or Property Manager

CERTIFICATE OF SERVICE

I hereby certify that a copy of the above notice was delivered to the above-named tenant on the _____ day of _____, 200__, by:

[ ] Personal delivery

[ ] Certified Mail

[ ] Posting on the premises

_____
Owner or Property Manager

SECURITY DEPOSIT REFUND SHEET

Tenant Name _____

Property Address _____

Move-out Date _____

Security Deposit Taken: $ _____

Deductions: _____
1. Cleaning   _____
2. Weeds   _____
3. Locks   _____
4. Rent   _____
5. Advertising   _____
6. Pest-infestation services   _____
7. Repairs   _____
   a. _____
   b. _____
   c. _____
8. Utilities   _____
9. Other   _____
10. Other   _____

Total Deductions: $ _____

Amount Refunded $ _____

Check # _____

Forwarding Address _____

_____

_____

TENANT MOVE-OUT SHEET

Tenant Name _____

Property Address _____

Date Moved-In_____   Rent at Time of Move In _____

Date Moved Out_____   Rent at Time of Move Out _____

Date Re-rented   _____   Amount Rented at_____

Reason for Moving _____

_____

30-day Notice given?   [ ] Yes   [ ] No

Forwarding Address:

_____

_____

_____

Security Deposit Taken _____

Amount Refunded_____

Comments: _____

_____

_____

_____

_____

_____

_____

_____

ADDENDUM

Additional Provisions attached to and made a part of the Purchase and Sales Agreement dated
on the property legally known as
Property
Between   (PURCHASER)
and   (SELLER)

NOTE: ONLY THE PARAGRAPHS CHECKED BELOW APPLY TO THIS CONTRACT:

TERMS AND CONDITIONS OF SALE

1.   **ASSUMPTION OF FIRST MORTGAGE:**
☐ Purchaser(s) shall assume and agree to pay an existing first mortgage held by:
in the approximate balance of $ at   % per annum payable at approximately $ per
month Including principal, interest, taxes and insurance in accordance with terms and conditions set forth therein. This mortgage is
freely assumable without qualification of escalation of interest rate.
☐ Purchaser(s) acknowledges this assumption requires qualification. Should Purchaser(s) nor qualify for said assumption, all monies on
deposit shall return to Purchaser(s) and this contract shall become null and void.
☐ Purchaser(s) acknowledges this assumption requires Escalation of the interest rate, and Qualification of Purchaser(s). Should
Purchaser(s) not qualify for said assumption, all monies on deposit shall be returned to Purchaser(s) and this contract shall become null
and void.
☐ Purchaser(s) to apply for said assumption within   working days upon acceptance of this contract.

2.   **ASSUMPTION OF SECOND MORTGAGE:**
Purchaser shall assume and agree to pay an existing second mortgage in the approximate amount of $ payable al approximately $
monthly. Said payment Includes principal
and interest at   % per annum.

3.   **NEW PURCHASE MONEY   MORTGAGE:**
Purchaser agrees to give a d Seller agrees to take a Purchase Money mortgage in the amount of $ payable at $ monthly,
Including principal and Interest al - %'per annum for   years.
Mortgage shall be prepare by Seller's attorney.

4.   **NEW INSTITUTIONAL   MORTGAGE:**
Purchasers to qualify for and obtain, at their own expense, a new conventional mortgage from a local lending institution or other institutional lender
in the amount of: (CIRCLE A B, C) A. $, B.   % of the purchase price, or C. Maximum amount available. Said mortgage
shall be at the prevailing interest rate for a minimum term of   years.
Purchasers shall apply for said mortgage within   working days of acceptance of this contract.

5.   **NEW FHA OR VA MORTGAGE ONLY:**
Purchaser to apply, qualify for, and obtain an ( ) FHA ( ) VA mortgage, insured by the FHA or guaranteed *by* VA at the prevailing FHA/VA rate of
interest effective at time of closing in an amount not less than $ for a period of approximately 30 years. Purchaser to
establish escrow account as required by Mortgagee for prepayment of taxes, hazard insurance, FHA Insurance as required by FHA, flood insurance if
required, and prepaid interest,   TO PAY PREVAILING MORTGAGE DISCOUNT AT TIME OF CLOSING NECESSARY TO
PLACE THE FHA/VA MORTGAGE. Mortgage closing costs, including (without limitation) mortgage title insurance, note documentary stamps,
intangible taxes, origination fee, recording fees, closing fees, survey, etc. to be paid at time of closing by   . Both Purchaser
and Seller agree to comply with FHA/VA commitment and regulations, and if FHA/VA requires any repairs or inspections to be made to the property
prior to closing, Seller agrees to pay for such repairs or inspections and have them made in a way as to meet the requirements of the FHA/VA
inspection. Appraisal fee to BE PAID FOR BY SELLER. Purchaser shall apply for said mortgage within   working days of acceptance
of this contract. The Buyer shall make a diligent, expeditious effort to secure said mortgage loan and any contrary efforts in this regard shall
constitute a breach of contract and forfeiture of deposit.
( ) FHA APPRAISAL: It is expressly agreed that, notwithstanding any other provisions of this contract, the Purchaser shall not be obligated to
complete the purchase of the property described herein or to incur any penalty by forfeiture of earnest money deposits or otherwise unless the Seller
has delivered to the Purchaser a written statement issued by the Federal Commissioner setting forth the appraised value of the property (excluding
closing costs) of not less than $, which statement the Seller hereby agrees to deliver to the Purchaser promptly after such appraised
value statement is made available to the Seller. The Purchaser shall, however, have the privilege and option of proceeding with the consummation of
the contract without regard to the amount of the appraised valuation made by the Federal Housing Commissioner. The appraised valuation is arrived
at to determine the maximum mortgage the Department of Housing and Urban Development will insure. HUD does not warrant the value or the
condition of the properly. The purchaser should satisfy himself/herself that the price and the condition of the properly are acceptable.
( ) VA APPRAISAL: It is expressly agreed that. notwithstanding any other provisions of this contract, the Purchaser shall not incur any penalty by
forfeiture of earnest money or otherwise or be obligated to complete the purchase of the property described herein, if the contract price or cost
exceeds the reasonable value of the property established by the Veterans Administration. The Purchaser shall, however, have the privilege and option

of proceeding with the consummation of this contract without regard to he amount of the reasonable value established by the Veterans Administration.

6.   MORTGAGE CONTINGENCY:
When so requested by the lending institution, Buyer shall comply with all the requirements of the mortgage commitment including the joinder of spouse in the mortgage documents, if requested. Buyer shall pay all loan costs including private mortgage insurance, if required. Repairs as required by the lending institutions shall be completed by the Seller, at his expense, prior to closing. If, after diligent effort on the part of the Purchaser, the Purchaser is unable to obtain and/or qualify for said mortgage(s) within   working days, all monies deposited hereunder shall be refunded (except for credit report) to Purchaser and parties herewith agree to enter into a Release of Purchase and Sale Contract, and the contract shall be declared null and void.

7.   BALANCE OF PURCHASE PRICE:
To be paid in Cash or Cashier's Check at the time of closing, all deposits to be a part thereof.

8.   CLOSING DATE:
Parties herein agree that the closing shall be on   or before if agreed by both parties. However, if lending institution is unable to close as scheduled, closing shall be postponed until lending institution can close.

9.   SPECIAL CLAUSE:

Having read the foregoing, I/we, the undersigned, hereby ratify, approve, accept, confirm, and acknowledge the same to be part of our Purchase Agreement.

WITNESSES AS TO PURCHASER: Date executed by Purchaser: _____

_____   _____ (SEAL)
                                                     (Purchaser)

_____   _____ (SEAL)
                                                     (Purchaser)

WITNESSES AS TO SELLER: Date executed by Purchaser: _____

_____   _____ (SEAL)
                                                     (Purchaser)

_____   _____ (SEAL)
                                                     (Purchaser)

Sent by Certified Mail,
Return receipt requested
_____ , 200_

NOTICE OF DISHONORED CHECK

TO: _____
    _____
    _____

CRIMINAL PENALTIES

You are hereby notified that a check, numbered _____, in the face amount of $_____, issued by
you on _____, 200_, drawn upon _____
and payable to _____, has been dishonored. Pursuant to
Florida law, you have 7 days from receipt of this notice to tender payment of the full amount of such
check plus a service charge of $25, if the face value does not exceed $50, $30, if the face value
exceeds $50 but does not exceed $300, $40, if the face value exceeds $300, or an amount of up to 5
percent of the face amount of the check, whichever is greater, the total amount due being $_____ and
_____ cents. Unless this amount is paid in full within the time specified above, the holder of such
check may turn over the dishonored check and all other available information relating to this incident to
the state attorney for criminal prosecution. You may be additionally liable in a civil action for triple the
amount of the check" but in no case less than $50, together with the amount of the check, a service
charge, court costs, reasonable attorney fees, and incurred bank fees, as provided in Chapter 68.065,
Florida Statutes.

CIVIL REMEDIES

You are hereby notified that a check numbered _____ in the face amount of $_____, issued by
you on _____, 200_, drawn upon _____ ,
and payable to_____, has been dishonored. Pursuant to
Florida law, you have 30 days from receipt of this notice to tender payment in cash of the full amount of the
check plus a service charge of $25, if the face value does not exceed $50, $30, if the face value exceeds $50
but does not exceed $30 , $40, if the face value exceeds $300, or 5 percent of the face amount of the check,
whichever is greater, the total amount due being $ _____ and _____ cents. Unless

this amount is paid in full within the 30-day period, the holder of the check or instrument may file a civil action
against you for three times the amount of the check, but in no case less than $50, in addition to the payment
of the check plus any court costs, reasonable attorney fees, and any bank fees incurred by the payee in taking the action.

NOTICE OF INTENTION TO IMPOSE CLAIM ON SECURITY DEPOSIT

Sent by Certified Mail, return receipt requested   ,200 .

A landlord must return a tenant's security deposit to the tenant no more than 30 days after the tenant leaves the leased property. The landlord may claim all or a portion of the security deposit only after giving the tenant written notice, by certified mail to the tenant's last known mailing address, of the landlord's intention to keep the deposit and the reason for keeping it. If the landlord does not send the notice within the 30 day period, the landlord cannot keep the security deposit. If the tenant does not object to the notice, the landlord may then keep the amount stated in the notice and must send the rest of the deposit to the tenant within 30 days after the date of the notice.

To:

Tenant's Name

Address

City/State/Zip

Date:

This is a notice of my intention to impose a claim for damages in the amount of $

upon your security deposit due to:

You are hereby notified that you must object in writing to this deduction from your security deposit within 30 days from the time you receive this notice or I will be authorized to deduct my claim from your security deposit. Your objection must be sent to:

Landlord's Name

Address

Phone Number:

LEAD-BASED PAINT OR LEAD-BASED PAINT HAZARD ADDENDUM

It is a condition of this contract that, until midnight of _____ , Buyer shall have the right to obtain a risk assessment or inspection of the Property for the presence of lead-based paint and/or lead-based paint hazards' at Buyer's expense. This contingency will terminate at that time unless Buyer or Buyer's agent delivers to the Seller or Seller's agent a written inspection , or risk assessment report listing the specific existing deficiencies and corrections needed, if any. If any corrections are necessary, Seller shall have the option of (i) completing them, (ii) providing for their completion, or (iii) refusing to complete them. If Seller elects not to complete or provide for completion of the corrections, then Buyer shall have the option of (iv) accepting the Property in its present condition, or (v) terminating this contract, in which case all earnest monies shall be refunded to Buyer. Buyer may waive the right to obtain a risk assessment or inspection of the Property for the presence of lead-based paint and/or lead based paint hazards at any time without cause.

*Intact lead-based paint that is in good condition is not necessarily a hazard. See EPA pamphlet "Protect Your Family From Lead in Your Home" for more information.

Disclosure of Information on Lead-Based Paint and Lead-Based Paint Hazards
Lead Warning Statement

Every Buyer of any interest in residential real property on which a residential dwelling was built prior to 1978 is notified that such property may present exposure to lead from lead-based paint that may place young children at risk of developing lead poisoning. Lead poisoning in young children may produce permanent neurological damage, including learning disabilities, reduced intelligence quotient, behavioral problems, and impaired memory. Lead poisoning also poses a particular risk to pregnant women. The Seller of any interest in residential real property is required to provide the Buyer with any information on lead-based paint hazards from risk assessments or inspections in the Seller's possession and notify the Buyer of any known lead-based paint hazards. A risk assessment or inspection for possible lead-based paint hazards is recommended prior to purchase.

Seller's Disclosure (initial)
    (a) Presence of lead-based paint and/or lead-based paint hazards (check one below):
    [ ] Known lead-based paint and/or lead-based paint hazards are present in the housing (explain).

    0 Seller has no knowledge of lead-based paint and/or lead-based paint hazards in the housing.
(b) Records and reports available to the Seller (check one below):
Seller has provided the Buyer with all available records and reports pertaining to lead-based paint and/or lead-based paint hazards in the housing (list documents below).

Seller has no reports or records pertaining to lead-based paint and/or lead-based paint hazards in the housing.

Buyer's Acknowledgment (initial)
    (c) Buyer has received copies of all information listed above.
    (d) Buyer has received the pamphlet *Protect Your Family from Lead in Your Home.*
    (e) Buyer has (check one below):
Received a 10-day opportunity (or mutually agreed upon period) to conduct a risk assessment or inspection
    the presence of lead-based paint and/or lead-based paint hazards; or
Waived the opportunity to conduct a risk assessment or inspection for the presence of lead-based paint and
    lead-based paint hazards.

Agent's Acknowledgment (initial)
    (f) Agent has informed the Seller of the Seller's obligations under 42 U.S.C. 4582(d) and is aware of his responsibility to ensure compliance.

(Continued – Next Page)

The following parties have reviewed the information above and certify, to the best of their knowledge, that the information provided by the signatory is true and accurate.

Buyer: _____ (SEAL) Date _____
Buyer: _____ (SEAL) Date _____
Agent: _____ (SEAL) Date _____
Seller: _____ (SEAL) Date _____
Seller: _____ (SEAL) Date _____
Agent: _____ (SEAL) Date _____

--[Space Above Reserved for Recording Purpose]--

WARRANTY DEED

THIS DEED made this _____ day of _____ between
_____ the Grantor, and
_____ the Grantee, whose address is
_____
_____

WITNESSETH, that the grantor, for and in consideration of the sum of TEN DOLLARS ($10.00), the receipt and sufficiency of which is hereby acknowledged and received, and for other good and valuable consideration, has granted, bargained, sold and conveyed, an by these presents does grant, bargain, sell, convey and confirm unto the grantee, their heirs and assigns forever, all the real property, together with improvements, if any, situate and being in the County of _____, State of _____ _____, described as follows:

Lot ____Block _____, City & County _____
Also known as street and number

_____
_____
_____
_____

TOGETHER with all and singular hereditaments and appurtenances thereunto belonging, or in anywise appertaining and the reversion and reversions, remainder and remainders, rents, issues, and profits thereof, and all the estate, right, title, interest, claim and demand whatsoever of the said grantor, either in law or equity, of, in and to the above bargained premises, with the hereditaments and appurtenances.

TO HAVE AND TO HOLD the said premises above bargained and described, with the appurtenances, unto the said grantee, their heirs and assigns forever. And the said grantor, for himself, his heirs, and personal representatives, does covenant, grant bargain and agree to and with the grantee, their heirs and assigns, that at the time of the ensealing and delivery of these presents, is well seized of the premises above conveyed, has good, sure, perfect, absolute indefeasible estate if inheritance, in law, in fee simple, and has good right, full power and lawful authority to grant, bargain, sell and convey the same in manner and form aforesaid, and that the same are free and clear from all former and other grants, bargains, sales, liens, taxes, assessments, encumbrances and restrictions of any kind or nature whatsoever, except any assessments, restrictions, covenants, zoning ordinances and rights-of-way of record and property taxes accruing subsequent to _____, a lien not yet due and payable.

The grantor shall and will WARRANT AND FOREVER DEFEND the above-bargained premises in the quiet and peaceable possession of the grantee, his heirs, and assigns, against all and every person or persons lawfully claiming the whole or any part thereof. The singular shall include the plural, the plural shall include the singular, and the use of any gender shall be applicable to all genders.

IN WITNESS WHEREOF, the grantor has executed this deed on the date set forth above.

STATE OF   COUNTY OF

_____
Grantor_____On _____before me,_____
_____ a notary public in and for said state personally appeared
_____
_____personally known to me
(or proved to me based upon satisfactory evidence) to be the person(s) whose
name(s) are subscribed to the within instrument and acknowledged that (s)he/they
executed the same in his/her/their signature on the instrument the person(s) or entity
on behalf of which they acted, executed the instrument.
Witness my hand and official seal

_____
NOTARY PUBLIC_____My commission expires _____

AUTHORIZATION TO RELEASE LOAN INFORMATION

Authorization dated this .._____

Borrower(s)_____

Loan No.: _____

Property: _____

TO: _____

        _____

        _____

I/We the undersigned hereby authorize you to release information regarding the above-referenced loan

to _____

and/or their agents/assigns. This form may be duplicated in blank and or sent via facsimile transmission.

This authorization is a continuation authorization for said persons to receive information about my loan,

including duplicates of any notices sent to me regarding my loan.

_____DOB:_____
Borrower   SSN: _____

_____DOB:_____
Borrower   SSN: _____

_____[Space Above Reserved for Recording Purposes]_____

QUIT-CLAIM DEED

THIS QUIT-CLAIM DEED, is executed this _____ day of _____, by

_____ hereinafter referred to as "First Party", to

_____ hereinafter referred to as "Second Party", whose

address is _____

WITNESSETH, that the First Party, for and in consideration of the sum of $10.00 and other good and valuable Consideration in hand. paid. by the said Second Party, the receipt whereof is hereby acknowledged, does hereby remise, release an quit claim unto the Second Party, all right, title, interest, and claim which the First Party has in and to the following described lot, piece, or parcel of land, situate, lying and being in the county of _____
_____ State of   to wit:

Lot   Block

Also known as street and number as _____

TO HAVE AND HOLD the same, together with all and singular the appurtenances thereunto, of all interest, equity and claim whatsoever the First Party may have, either in law or equity, for the proper use, benefit and behalf of the Second Party forever.

IN WITNESS HEREOF, the First Party has signed and sealed these presents the day and year first above written.

_____   _____
First Party   First Party

STATE OF _____ COUNTY OF _____

On_____, before me _____, a notary public in and for said state
personally appeared   personally known to me (or proved to me based upon satisfactory
evidence) to be the person(s) whose name(s) are subscribed to the within instrument and acknowledged that (s)he/they executed the
same in his/her/their signature on the instrument the person(s) or entity on behalf of which they acted, executed the instrument.

Witness my hand and official seal

_____
NOTARY PUBLIC II
            My commission expires _____[NOTARY SEAL]

GLOSSARY

Abstract of Title. A compilation of the recorded documents relating to a parcel of land, from which an attorney may give an opinion as to the condition of title. Also known in some states as a *preliminary title report.*

Acceleration. A condition in a financing instrument giving the lender the power to declare all sums owed the lender immediately due and payable upon an event such as sale of the property.

Acre. An area that contains 43,560 square feet of land. Also known as a *due-on-sale.*

Acknowledgement. A declaration made by a person signing a document before a notary public or other officer.

Addendum. An addition to a contract or agreement that adds more provisions or modifies provisions of the contract or agreement.

Adjustment. Increase or decrease in the sale price of a comparable property to account for a feature that the property has or does not have in comparison to the subject property.

Adverse Possession. Most states have laws that permit someone to claim ownership of property that is occupied for a number of years. This is common where a fence is erected over a boundary line (called an *encroachment*) without the objection of the rightful owner. After a number of years, the person who erected the fence may be able to commence a court proceeding to claim ownership of the property.

Agency. A relationship in which the agent is given the authority to act on behalf of another person.

All-Inclusive Deed of Trust. See *wraparound mortgage.*

ALTA. American Land Title Association.

Amortize. To reduce a debt by regular payments of both principal and interest.

Appraised Value. The value of a property at a given time, based on facts regarding the location, improvements, etc., of the property and surroundings.

Appreciation. An increase in the net value of real estate.

Appurtenance. Anything attached to the land or used with it, passing to the new owner upon sale.

ARM. An adjustable-rate mortgage; that is, a loan whose interest rate may adjust over time depending on certain factors or a predetermined formula.

Arrears. Payment made after its due date and is in arrears. Interest is said to be paid in arrears because it is paid to the date of payment rather than in advance.

Assignment of Contract. A process by which a person sells, transfers, and/or assigns rights under an agreement. Often used in the context of the assignment of a purchase contract by a buyer, or the assignment of a lease by a tenant.

Assumable Loan. A loan secured by a mortgage or deed of trust containing no due-on-sale provision. Most pre-1989 FHA loans and pre-1988 VA loans are assumable without qualification. Some newer loans may be assumed with the express permission of the note holder.

Assumption of Mortgage. Agreement by a buyer to assume the liability under an existing note secured by a mortgage or deed of trust.

Bankruptcy. A provision of federal law whereby a debtor surrenders assets to the bankruptcy court and is relieved of the obligation to repay unsecured debts. After bankruptcy, the debtor is discharged, and unsecured creditors may not pursue further collection efforts against him or her. Secured creditors continue to be secured by property but may not take other action to collect.

Balloon Mortgage. A note calling for periodic payments that are insufficient to fully amortize the face amount of the note prior to maturity, so that a principal sum known as a *balloon* is due at maturity.

Basis. The financial interest one has in a property for tax purposes. Basis is adjusted down by depreciation and up by capital improvements.

Beneficiary. One for whose benefit trust property is held. Also known as the lender under a deed of trust.

Binder. A report issued by a title insurance company setting forth the condition of title and setting forth conditions that, if satisfied, will cause a policy of title insurance to be issued. Also know as a *title commitment*.

Building Restriction Line. A required set-back a certain distance from the road within which no building may take place. This restriction may appear in the original subdivision plat, in restrictive covenants, or by building codes and zoning ordinances.

Buyer's Agent. A real estate broker or agent who represents the buyer's interests, though typically the fee is a split of the listing broker's commission. Also known as the *selling agent*.

Capital Gain. Profit from the sale of a capital asset, such as real property. A long-term capital gain is a gain derived from property had more than twelve months. Long-term gains can be taxed at lower rates than short-term gains.

Caveat Emptor. Buyer beware. A seller is under no obligation to disclose defects, but may not actively conceal a known defect or lie if asked.

Certificate of Occupancy. A certificate issued by a local governmental body stating that the building may be occupied.

Chain of Title. The chronological order of conveyancing of a parcel of land, from the original owner to the present owner.

Closing. The passing of a deed or mortgage, signifying the end of a sale or mortgage of real property. Also known in some areas as *passing papers* or *closing of escrow.* A meeting between the buyer, seller, and lender, or their agent, where the property and funds legally change hands.

Closing Costs. Expenses incurred in the closing of a real estate or mortgage transaction. Most fees are associated with the buyer or borrower's loan. Closing costs typically include an origination fee, discount points, appraisal fee, title search and insurance, survey, taxes, deed recording fee, credit report, and notary fees.

Cloud on Title. An uncertainty, doubt, or claim against the rights of the owner of a property, such as a recorded purchase contract or option. Any evidence of encumbrances.

Commitment. A written promise to make or insure a loan for a specified amount and on specified items. Also used in the context of title insurance *(title commitment)*.

Community Property. In community property states (Arizona, California, Idaho, Louisiana, Nevada, New Mexico, Texas, Washington, Wisconsin), all property of husband and wife acquired after the marriage is presumed to belong to both, regardless of how it is titled.

Comparables. Properties used as comparisons to determine the value of a specified property.

Condominium. A structure of two or more units, the interior spaces of which are individually owned. The common areas are owned as tenants in common by the condominium owners, and ownership is restricted by an association. A system of individual ownership of portions or units in a multiunit structure, combined with joint ownership of common areas. Each individual may sell or encumber his or her own unit.

Contingency. The dependence on a stated event that must occur before a contract is binding. Used both in the context of a loan and a contract of sale.

Contract of Sale. A bilateral (two-way) agreement wherein the seller agrees to sell and buyer agrees to buy a certain parcel of land, usually with improvements. Also used in reference to an installment land contract.

Counteroffer. A rejection of a seller's offer, usually with an amended agreement to sell the property to the potential buyer on different terms from the original offer.

Condemnation. A judicial proceeding through which a governmental body takes ownership of a private property for a public use.

Collateral. Property that is pledged to secure a loan.

Conventional Mortgage. A loan neither insured by the FHA nor guaranteed by the VA.

Contract. A legally enforceable agreement between two or more parties.

Cooperative Apartment. A cooperative is a corporation that holds title to the land and building. Each co-op owner has shares of stock in the corporation that corresponds to an equivalent proprietary lease of an apartment space. Co-ops were very popular in New York City at one time, but are less common because of their lack of marketability due to high association fees.

Credit Report. A report documenting the credit history and current status of a person's credit.

Deficiency. The difference between the amount owed to a note holder and the proceeds received from a foreclosure sale. The lender may, in some states, obtain a *deficiency judgment* against the borrower for the difference.

Delivery. The transfer of a deed to the grantee so that the grantor may not revoke it. A deed, signed but held by the grantor, does not pass title.

Depreciation. Decrease in value to real property improvements caused by deterioration or obsolescence.

Documentary Tax Stamps. Stamps, affixed to a deed, showing the amount of transfer tax. Some states simply charge the transfer tax without affixing stamps. Also known as *doc stamps.*

Double Closing. A closing wherein a property is bought and then sold simultaneously. Also called *double escrow* and *flipping.*

Due-on-Sale Clause. A provision in a mortgage or deed of trust that gives the lender the option to require payment in full of the indebtedness on transfer of title to the property (or any interest therein).

Earnest Money. A good faith deposit or down payment.

Easement. An interest that one has in the land of another. May be created by grant, reservation, agreement, prescription, or necessary implication.

Eminent Domain. A constitutional right for a governmental authority to acquire private property for public use by condemnation, and the payment of just compensation.

Encroachment. Construction or imposition of a structure onto the property of another.

Encumbrance. A claim, lien, or charge against real property.

Equity. The difference between the market value of the property and the homeowner's mortgage debt.

Equitable Title. The interest of the purchase under an installment land contract.

Escrow. Delivery of a deed by a grantor to a third party for delivery to the grantee on the happening of a contingent event.

Escrow Agent, Escrow Company. Individual or company that performs closing services for real estate loans and sales transactions.

Escrow Payment. That portion of a borrower's monthly payment held in trust by the lender to pay for taxes, mortgage insurance, hazard insurance, lease payments, and other items as they become due. Also known as *impounds*.

Estate. From the English feudal system, this defines the extent of one' ownership in a property.

Estate for Years. An estate limited to a term of years. An estate for years is commonly called a *lease*. On the expiration of the estate for years, the property reverts back to the former owner.

Fee Simple. The highest form of ownership. An estate under which the owner is entitled to unrestricted powers to dispose of the property, and which can be left by will or inherited. Also known as *fee* or *fee simple absolute*.

Federal Housing Administration (FHA). A federal agency that insures first mortgages, enabling lenders to loan a very high percentage of the sale price.

Fixture. An item of personal property attached to real property.

Freddie Mac (FHLMC). Federal Home Loan Mortgage Corporation.

Foreclosure. A proceeding to extinguish all rights, title, and interest of the owner(s) of property in order to sell the property to satisfy a lien against it. About half of the states use a mortgage foreclosure, which is a lawsuit in court. About half use a power of sale proceeding, which is dictated by a deed of trust and is usually less time-consuming.

Ginnie Mae (GNMA). Government National Mortgage Association. A federal association working with FHA that offers special assistance in obtaining mortgages, and purchases mortgages in a secondary capacity.

Good Faith Estimate. A lender's estimate of closing costs and monthly payment required by RESPA.

Grant Deed. A deed commonly used in California to convey title. By law, a grant deed gives certain warranties of title.

Grantee. A person receiving an interest in property.

Grantor. A person granting or giving up an interest in property.

Grantor/Grantee Index. The most common document recording indexing system is by grantor (the person conveying an interest, usually the seller or mortgagor) and grantee (the person receiving an interest, usually the buyer or mortgagee). All documents conveying property or an interest therein (deed, mortgage, lease, easement, etc.) are recorded by the grantor's last name in the grantor index. The same transaction is cross-indexed by the grantee's last name in the grantee index.

Heirs and Assigns. Words usually found in a contract or deed that indicate that the obligations assumed or interest granted or binding upon or insure to benefit of the heirs or assigns of the party.

Highest and Best Use. The use of land that produces the highest property value.

Homeowners Association. An association of people who own homes in a given area for the purpose of improving or maintaining the quality of the area. Also used in the context of a condominium association.

Impound Account. Account held by a lender for payment of taxes, insurance, or other payments. Also known as an *escrow* account.

Installment Land Contract. The ILC is an agreement wherein the buyer makes payments in a manner similar to a mortgage. The buyer has equitable title. However, the seller holds legal title to the property until the contract is paid off. The buyer has equitable title, and, for all intents and purposes, is the owner of the property. Also known as a *contract for deed* or *contract of sale.*

Installment Sale. A sale that involves the seller receiving payments over time. The Internal Revenue Code contains specific definitions and promulgates specific rules concerning installment sales and tax treatment of them. Also known as an *owner carry* sale.

Insured Mortgage. A mortgage insured against loss to the mortgagee in the event of default and failure of the mortgaged property to satisfy the balance owing plus costs of foreclosure.

Interest Rate. The percentage of an amount of money that is paid for its use for a specified time.

Joint and Several Liability. A liability that allows a creditor to collect against any one of the debtors for the entire amount of the debt, regardless of fault or culpability. Most mortgage notes that are signed by husband and wife create joint and several liability.

Joint Tenancy. An undivided interest in property, taken by two or more joint tenants. The interests must equal, accruing under the same conveyance, and beginning at the same time. On death of a joint tenant, the interest passes to the surviving joint tenants, rather than to the heirs of the deceased.

Judgment. The decision of a court of law. Money judgments, when recorded, become a lien on real property of the defendant.

Junior Mortgage. Mortgage of lesser priority than the previously recorded mortgage.

Land Lease. Owners of property will sometimes give long-term leases of land up to ninety-nine years. A lease of more than ninety-nine years is considered a transfer of fee simple. Land leases are commonly used to build banks, car lots, and shopping malls.

Land Trust. A revocable, living trust primarily used to hold title to real estate for privacy and anonymity. Also known as an *Illinois land trust* or *nominee trust.* The land trustee is a nominal title holder, with the beneficiaries having the exclusive right to direct and control the actions of the trustee.

Lease/Option. An agreement by which the lessee (tenant) has the unilateral option to purchase the leased premises from the lessor (landlord). Some lease/option agreements provide for a portion of the rent to be applied toward the purchase price. The price may be fixed at the beginning of the agreement or be determined by another formula, such as an appraisal at a later time. Also referred to as a *lease/purchase.*

Lease Purchase. Often used interchangeably with the expression *lease/option,* but technically means a lease in conjunction with a bilateral purchase agreement. Often used by real estate agents to mean a purchase agreement whereby the tenant takes possession prior to close of escrow.

Legal Description. A statement describing a particular property by a standard method determined by law.

Lien. An encumbrance against property for money, either voluntary (e.g., mortgage), involuntary (e.g., judgment), or by operation of law (e.g., property tax lien).

Life Estate. An estate in real property for the life of a living person. The estate then reverts back to the grantor or to a third party.

Lis Pendens. A legal notice recorded to show pending litigation relating to real property and giving notice that anyone acquiring an interest in said property subsequent to the date of the notice may be bound by the outcome of the litigation. Often filed prior to mortgage foreclosure proceeding.

License. An authority to perform a particular act or series of acts upon the land of another without possessing any estate or interest therein (e.g., a ski lift ticket). A license is similar to an easement in that it gives someone permission to cross property for a specific purpose. An easement is a property interest, whereas a license is a contractual right.

Liquidated Damages. A contract clause that limits a party to a certain sum in lieu of actual damages. In the case of a real estate purchase and sale contract, the seller's legal remedy is limited to the buyer's earnest money deposit.

Loan-to-Value Ratio. The ratio of the mortgage loan amount to the property's appraised value (or the selling price, whichever is less).

Multiple Listing Service. A service performed by the Local Board of Realtors® that provides information to aid in the sale of properties to a wide market base.

Notary Public. One authorized by law to acknowledge and certify documents and signatures as valid.

Note. A written promise to repay a certain sum of money on specified terms. Also known as a *promissory note*.

Offer. A proposal to buy.

Option. The unilateral right to do something. For example, the right to renew a lease or purchase a property. The optionee is the holder of the option. The optionor is the grantor of the option. The optionor is bound by the option, but the optionee is not.

Origination Fee. A fee or charge for work involved in the evaluation, preparation, and submission of a proposed mortgage loan. Usually about one percent of the loan amount.

Payoff Amount. A total amount needed to satisfy full payment on an existing loan or lien.

Performance Mortgage. A mortgage or deed of trust given to secure performance of an obligation other than a promissory note.

Periodic Tenancy. An estate from week-to-week, month-to-month, etc. In the absence of a written agreement (or on the expiration of lease once payments are accepted), a periodic tenancy is created. Either party can terminate this type of arrangement by giving notice, usually equal to the amount of the period, or as prescribed by state law.

Personal Property. Items which are removable and not part of the real property.

PITI. Principal, interest, taxes, and insurance.

Plat. A map showing the division of a piece of land.

Points. Fee paid by a borrower to obtain a loan. A point is one percent of the principal amount of the loan. The borrower may usually pay more points to reduce the interest rate of the loan.

Power of Attorney. A written document authorizing another to act on one's behalf as an attorney in fact.

Prepayment Penalty. An additional charge imposed by the lender for paying off a loan before its due date.

Probate. A court process to prove a will is valid.

Promissory Note. A written, unsecured note promising to pay a specified amount of money on demand, often transferable to a third party.

Prorate. To divide in proportionate shares. Used in the context of a closing, at which such things as property taxes, interest, rents, and other items are adjusted in favor of the seller, buyer, or lender.

Purchase Agreement A binding agreement between parties for the purchase of real estate.

Purchase Money Mortgage. A loan obtained in conjunction with the purchase of real estate.

Quiet Title Proceeding. A court action to establish or clear up uncertainty as to ownership to real property. Often required if a lien or cloud appears on title that cannot be resolved.

Quit Claim Deed. A deed by which the grantor gives up any claim he or she may have in the property. Often used to clear up a cloud on title.

Real Estate. Land and anything permanently affixed to the land, and those things attached to the buildings.

Real Property. Land and whatever by nature or artificial annexation is attached to it.

Realtor®. Any member of the National Association of Realtors®.

Recording. The act of publicly filing a document, such as a deed or mortgage.

Recourse Note. A note under which the holder can look personally to the borrower for payment.

Redemption. The right, in some states, for an owner or lien holder to satisfy the indebtedness due on a mortgage in foreclosure after sale.

Refinancing. The repayment of a loan from the proceeds of a new loan using the same property as collateral.

Reissue Rate. A discounted charge for a title insurance policy if a previous policy on the same property was issued within a specified period (usually three to five years).

Release. An instrument releasing a lien or encumbrance (e.g., mortgage) from a property.

Reproduction Cost. The current cost of reconstructing an exact duplicate of the subject property.

RESPA (Real Estate Settlement Procedures Act). A federal law requiring disclosure of certain costs in the sale of residential property that is to be financed by a federally insured lender. Also requires that the lender provide a good faith estimate of closing costs prior to closing of the loan.

Room to wriggle. Delayed time on any ongoing process strategy to overcome opposition.

Second Mortgage. A loan secured by a mortgage or trust deed, which lien is junior to a first mortgage or deed of trust.

Secondary Mortgage Market. The buying and selling of first mortgages and deeds of trust by banks, insurance companies, government agencies, and other mortgagees.

Security Instrument. A document under which collateral is pledged (e.g., mortgage).

Settlement Statement. A statement prepared by a closing agent (usually a title or escrow company) giving a complete breakdown of costs and charges involved in a real estate transaction. Required by RESPA on a form HUD-I.

Special Assessment. Tax imposed by the local government for public improvements, such as new streets.

Special Warranty Deed. A seller warrants he or she has done nothing to impair title but makes no warranty prior to his or her ownership.

Specific Performance. An action to compel the performance of a contract.

Subdivision. Dividing land into lots and streets, typically under strict requirements of the state and county.

Sublet. To let part of one's estate in a lease. A subtenant is not in privity of contract with the landlord and neither can look to each for performance of a lease agreement.

Subject-To. When transferring title to a property encumbered by a mortgage lien without paying off the debt or assuming the note, the buyer is taking title "subject to."

Subordination. The process by which a lien holder agrees to permit a lien to become junior or subordinate to another lien.

Tenancy in Common. With tenancy in common, each owner (called a *tenant*) has an undivided interest in the possession of the property. Each tenant's interest is saleable and transferable. Each tenant can convey that interest by deed, mortgage or will. Joint ownership is presumed to be in common if nothing further is stated on the deed.

Tenancy by the Entirety. A form of ownership recognized in some states by which husband and wife each own the entire property. As with joint tenancy, in event of death of one, the survivor owns the property without probate. In some states, tenancy by entirety protects the property from obligations of one spouse.

Testate. When a person dies with a will.

Title. Title is the evidence of ownership. In essence, title is more important than ownership because having proper title is proof of ownership. If you have a problem with your title, you will have trouble proving your ownership and thus selling or mortgaging your property.

Title Insurance. An insurance policy that protects the insured (purchaser and/or lender) against loss arising from defects in title. A policy protecting the lender is called a *loan policy,* whereas a policy protecting the purchaser is called an *owner's policy.* Virtually all transactions involving a loan require title insurance.

Title Search. An examination of the public records to disclose facts concerning the ownership of real estate.

Truth in Lending. Federal law requiring, among other things, a disclosure of interest rate charges and other information about a loan.

Trust. A right to or in property held for the benefit of another, which may be written or implied.

Trustee. One who holds property in trust for another party.

Trustor. One who creates a trust by granting property to a trustee. Also known as the *borrower* on a deed of trust.

VA Loan. A long-term, low or no down-payment loan guaranteed by the Department of Veterans Affairs, which is offered to individuals qualified by military service or other entitlements.

Warranty Deed. A deed under which the seller makes a guarantee or warranty that title is marketable and will defend all claims against it.

Wraparound Mortgage. A mortgage that is subordinate to and incorporates the terms of an underlying mortgage. The mortgagor (borrower) makes payments to the mortgagee (lender), who then makes payments on an underlying mortgage. Also referred to as an *all-inclusive deed of trust* in some states.

Yield Spread Premium. A kickback from the lender to the mortgage broker for the additional profit made from marking up the interest rate on a loan.

Zoning. Regulation of private land use and development by a local government.

INDEX

A

Accessibility: 2
Advertising: 61, 64, 77
Agent: 31, 76, 87, 135, 137
Anxious seller: 41
Applications: 28, 30, 64
Appreciation: 23, 25
As is rider: 93
Ask questions: 48, 49
Assets: 20, 43, 53, 109, 111
Assumption: 17
Attitude of the mind: 9
Attorney: 28, 42, 88, 91, 108, 110, 142
Attractive features: 79
Auctions: 39
Avoid being ripped off: 86

B

Bad breaks: 3
Bankers: 53, 55
Bargain deals: 25
Bathroom: 80, 104
Behavior: 10
Being lucky: 6
Believe: 1, 2
Bending the rules: 4
Best deal: 28-30, 80
Best terms: 52
Body language: 67

Buy low sell high: 75
Buy the right property: 38
Buyer investor: 14
Buying strategies: 17

C

Can you fix it?: 42
Capital assets: 1
Capital resources: 35
Cash flow: 6, 16, 23, 25, 26, 59, 69, 71,
    72, 75, 76, 80, 96-98
Closing agent: 87, 90, 91
Closing the transaction: 87
Collection: 96
Compile documents: 28
Complaints: 85
Condominium rider: 92
Contingent clause: 101, 105
Create your own luck: 6
Credit bag: 31
Credit check: 64, 67
Credit fix: 32
Credit score: 32-34
Curb appeal: 39, 42, 77, 83

D

Dealing with lenders: 29
Deposit: 63-65, 92
Depreciation: 24, 137
Design: 15

Discipline: 9, 27
Disclosure rider: 92
Distressed owner: 40
Donald Trump: 46, 97
Done deal: 7
Dress: 7

E

Earl Nightingale: 9
Easy qualifying: 17
Effective management: 95
Equity: 23, 39, 137
Equity buildup: 23, 25, 80
Ernest money: 92, 137
Escrow fund: 92
Establish a business address: 71
Estate sale: 39
Evidence of title: 88
Exceptions: 89
Exclusions in title: 88, 89

F

Face to face: 47
Farm area: 31
Finder's fee: 63
Finding a contractor: 42
Finding the best loan: 29
First impression: 6, 7
First mortgage: 7, 16, 19, 82
First to mention: 50
Fix credit glitches: 31
Flipping: 81, 137
Focus: 1, 8, 80
Focus on what you like: 37

G

George Jennings: 16
Get ready: 32, 53
Getting established: 97
Getting started: 1, 107
Goals: 5, 8, 27
God is with you: 4
Good environment: 96

Good tenants: 96, 99

H

Handyman: 43, 73, 98
Hard money lenders: 55
Homeowner: 56
Hope: 1
How much money do you need?: 56
HUD-1: 85, 90

I

Improvements: 23, 59, 73
Inspection kit: 65
Inspections: 22, 98, 101
Insulation rider: 93
Insurance: 21, 88, 89, 99, 100, 144
Investing in real estate: 4, 14, 25, 53
IRA 401(k): 14, 109

J

J.P. Morgan: 1

K

Kitchen remodeling: 80
Know the manager: 55
Knowledge: 14

L

Lead base paint rider: 93
Lease: 64, 72, 99, 140
Lender: 18, 19, 28-30, 40, 55, 82, 89, 90
Less cash for down payment: 16, 49, 59
Leverage: 35
Liabilities: 53
Lifetime or lump sum?: 18
Listing agent: 31, 78
Little or no cash down: 57
Loan package: 89
Location: 37
Low balling settlement: 85
Lowest mortgage rate: 30
LTV (loan to value): 17

M

Mailing address: 70
Maintenance: 97, 98
Manage the right way: 97
Markups: 85, 86
Military newspaper: 62
Mortgage broker: 28, 32
Motivation: 10, 11
Motives: 10, 49

N

Name dropping: 6
National Association of Realtors: 14, 42
National credit bureaus: 32, 34
Negative desires: 52
Negotiate with seller: 39, 51
Net operating income: 26, 54
Newspaper: 61, 62
No money down: 19, 56, 57
No monthly payment: 18

O

One year: 17
Opinion of title: 88
Opportunity: 5, 9, 76
Other people's money: 14, 16, 35, 56
Overcome psychological flaws: 3

P

Payoff letter: 89
Personality: 47
Picture your goals: 1
Pictures: 66
Planning and dreaming: 1
Pre-rental check: 98
Predatory lending: 87
Prepare for management: 95
Price and terms: 39, 49
Proofreading closing package: 90
Property address: 62
Proven path: 1

Q

Quality of life: 20
Questions to ask seller: 38, 47-49

R

Real estate agent: 76, 78
Receipts: 98
Renovation: 43, 71, 78
Rent collection: 96
Rentals in the area: 38
Retirement future: 107
Reverse mortgage: 18, 19
Room to wriggle: 51, 71, 80, 105, 143

S

Sale by owner: 31, 41
Sales contract: 91
Savings: 19, 24
Scarcity: 5, 8
Self-esteem: 2, 7
Sell yourself first: 35
Sigmund Freud: 3
Small details: 78
Small investors: 15
Smile: 8
Stocks and bonds: 69
Successful investors: 8
Super fat-cats: 7
Super poor: 7
Support: 27, 35

T

Tenants pay upkeep: 99
Think positive: 2
Thomas Carlyle: 9
Title: 87, 88, 133, 135, 137, 144
Title insurance: 88, 144
Title search: 87, 144
Trapeze artist: 36

U

Unlimited markups: 86

Unseen current: 5
Upcharges/markups: 85
Use several banks: 55
Use your vision: 50

V

VA Mortgage: 17
VA/FHA rider: 92
Value increase: 96

W

Warranty deed: 91, 143, 145
Weakness: 46
When you pray: 2
William James: 9

Y

Your coach: 10
Your ego: 3
Your own flair: 79
Your style: 46